MORE
OUTBOUND JOURNEYS
IN PENNSYLVANIA

A Keystone Book is so designated to distinguish it from the typical scholarly monograph that a university press publishes. It is a book intended to serve the citizens of Pennsylvania by educating them and others, in an entertaining way, about aspects of the history, culture, society, and environment of the state as part of the Middle Atlantic region.

MORE OUTBOUND JOURNEYS IN PENNSYLVANIA

A Guide to Natural Places for Individual and Group Outings

MARCIA BONTA

A Keystone Book

The Pennsylvania State University Press
University Park, Pennsylvania

Photographs by Bruce Bonta

Maps by Deasy GeoGraphics Laboratory, Department of Geography,
The Pennsylvania State University

Library of Congress Cataloging-in-Publication Data

Bonta, Marcia, 1940–
    More outbound journeys in Pennsylvania : a guide to natural places for
    individual and group outings / Marcia Bonta.

          p.   cm.
    Continues: Outbound journeys in Pennsylvania.
    "A Keystone book."
    Includes bibliographical references (p.   )
    ISBN 0-271-01444-X (cloth)
    ISBN 0-271-01445-8 (paper)
    1. Hiking—Pennsylvania—Guidebooks.   2. Pennsylvania—Guidebooks.
    I. Bonta, Marcia, 1940–   Outbound journeys in Pennsylvania.
    II. Title.
    GV199.42.P4B65   1995
    796.5'1'09748—dc20   94-23946
                                                                      CIP

Second printing, 1999

Published by the Pennsylvania State University Press,
University Park, PA 16802-1003

It is the policy of The Pennsylvania State University Press to use acid-free paper
for the first printing of all clothbound books. Publications on uncoated stock
satisfy the minimum requirements of American National Standard for
Information Sciences—Permanence of Paper for Printed Library Materials,
ANSI Z39.48–1992.

To my husband, Bruce,
best friend and companion on all my Outbound Journeys,
who shares my love for Pennsylvania's natural places.

CONTENTS

ACKNOWLEDGMENTS

Many people helped in my search for new places to write about and suggested their own favorites. Others answered questions and gave me additional information. Still others guided my husband, Bruce, and me through some of these special areas. I would especially like to thank Evelyn Anderson, Mark Arbogast, Jean Aron, Jim Bashline, Tad Beck, Marilyn Black, Ed Brucker, Cal Butchkoski, Ed Cameron, George Carmichael, Dan Comoroski, Bud Cook, Chris Dooley, Bill Ettinger, Paula Ford, Roy Gilham, Hal Greenlee, Chip and Ralph Harrison, Ellen Hearn, David Ide, Claudia James, Larry H. Klotz, Randy Kraft, Roger Latham, Bob Leberman, Robert Mowrer, Guy and Nancy Mullen, Bob Mulvihill, Bob Myers, Jim Nelson, Pat Pingel, Bob Pitcavage, Bill Randour, Chris Reese, Mike and Noreen Sankovitch, Katherine Shelly, Greg Smith, Jean and Jim Stull, Kim Van Fleet, Don Wary, and Jeremy Woodhouse. I also thank my editor at *Pennsylvania Wildlife*, Jack Hubley. Nearly all of these chapters appeared in different form in *Pennsylvania Wildlife* (1988–1995) except for "Conneaut Marsh," which was published in *Boat Pennsylvania* (Summer 1992).

As usual, my husband accompanied me on all but one of my journeys. He also took all but one of the photographs and wrote the directions. Without his help and support, this book could not have been written.

SOURCES

You must have a good road map of Pennsylvania to follow the directions in this book. The State Parks Recreational Guide Map, prepared by the Bureau of State Parks, is excellent and contains recreational information about all of Pennsylvania's state parks. State parks, as well as state forests, natural and wild areas, state game lands, and national parks, are clearly marked on the map. To get a complimentary copy, write to the Bureau of State Parks, P.O. Box 8551, Harrisburg, PA 17105, or call 1-800-63PARKS or 717-787-6640.

For more information on state parks, including free maps and brochures on individual parks, call the above numbers or write to the Bureau of State Parks. Another source of free information about Pennsylvania's state parks is the *Pennsylvania State Parks* magazine, published quarterly and available free of charge from the Bureau of State Parks.

The Pennsylvania Atlas & Gazetteer, published by the DeLorme Mapping Company, P.O. Box 298, Freeport, ME 04032 (or call 207-865-4171), is sold in many bookstores and on newsstands. We never go anywhere without it.

The *Pennsylvania Trail Guide,* published in 1989 by the Department of Environmental Resources, lists more than 800 trails for hiking, biking, skiing, horseback-riding, snowmobiling, canoeing, and ATVs and is for sale at state park offices.

An informational brochure (with map) highlighting 37 projects of the Western Pennsylvania Conservancy, 12 of which are featured in this book, is available free for those who join the Conservancy. In addition, the Conservancy publishes several brief outing guides a year, also available free to members. For more information, write to the Western Pennsylvania Conservancy, 316 Fourth Avenue, Pittsburgh, PA 15222. Their newsletter, *Conserve,* keeps members up-to-date on new purchases and activities at several nature centers.

The Pennsylvania Chapter of The Nature Conservancy at 1211 Chestnut Street, 12th Floor, Philadelphia, PA 19107-4122, also has an informative members' newsletter, *Penns Woods,* and a booklet that highlights 21 of the 35 places they have saved in eastern Pennsylvania.

To get free state forest public-use maps, with a limit of six maps per request, write to the Department of Environmental Resources, Bureau of Forestry, Box 8552, Harrisburg, PA 17105-8552, or call 717-783-7941.

The Pennsylvania Game Commission sells an Outdoor Recreation Map for each of its six field regions: Northwest, Southwest, North-Central, South-Central, Northeast, and Southeast. The 24-by-36-inch multicolor maps, made of tear-resistant and water-repellent material, highlight state game lands, state forests and parks, and properties enrolled in the agency's public-access programs. These maps also include 100-foot contour lines and show roads, towns, and waterways. Write to the Pennsylvania Game Commission, Department MS, 2001 Elmerton Avenue, Harrisburg, PA 17110-9797. Individual maps of each state game land are available from the regional office for a small fee.

Other sources of information on natural Pennsylvania are the *Pennsylvania Game News,* published monthly by the Pennsylvania Game Commission, and *Pennsylvania Wildlife,* published bimonthly by the Pennsylvania Wildlife Federation. For *Game News* subscription information, write to the Pennsylvania Game Commission at the address given above. To join the Pennsylvania Wildlife Federation and receive *Pennsylvania Wildlife,* write to the Federation at 2426 North Second Street, Harrisburg, PA 17110.

The Selected Bibliography at the end of this book provides additional sources of invaluable information.

INTRODUCTION

When I finished writing the first book, *Outbound Journeys in Pennsylvania*, I thought I had covered most, if not all, of the best natural places in the commonwealth. How wrong I was! Because I planned to continue my "Outbound Journeys" column for *Pennsylvania Wildlife*, which I began in 1983, I kept searching for new places—and finding them. Not only had I missed a few the first time around, but more and more new areas were being purchased both by state agencies and by nongovernmental organizations.

This growing awareness of Pennsylvania's natural heritage, along with an increasing number of people willing to support new purchases of public lands and to join private land conservancies, nature centers, and sanctuaries, is an encouraging development that shows no signs of slowing down. For instance, the Pennsylvania Bureau of Forestry recently designated 18 new natural areas, bringing the total to 62. They also added 2 wild areas to the 13 existing ones. The Pennsylvania Game Commission continues to buy large tracts of land, often brokered through the land conservancies, and the Bureau of State Parks has designated a new natural-areas program to protect areas of "unique scenic, geologic, or ecological value."

Nongovernmental organizations interested in land conservation are also growing in number. In addition to the Western Pennsylvania Conservancy and the Pennsylvania Chapter of The Nature Conservancy, both of which have purchased land not only to resell to local, county, and state government agencies but also to retain as research sites, there are more locally based groups. Good examples are the Lancaster County Conservancy and the Heritage Conservancy, which are helping to preserve Pennsylvania's natural heritage for all the citizens of the commonwealth. Then there are the organizations formed simply to save and maintain a single place. All these and more are covered in this book.

The variety of areas covered in this new book will appeal to people of all ages, just as my first book did. There are state game lands, state parks, wild and natural areas, nature centers, and private organization properties, all of which have special characteristics—such as unusual or abundant wildlife, rare wildflowers, unique geological formations, old-growth forests, or endangered ecosystems. To reach three of these places, it is necessary to use a canoe, but you needn't be an expert canoeist. Most of the outings are not too strenuous, since I am somewhat past the half-century mark and a rambler rather than a hiker.

I also recognize, from reader feedback on my first book, that there are many displaced Pennsylvanians throughout the United States who are eager to read about their home state even though they can't visit. For those and others who are unable to travel, I have tried to make this book more than a guidebook. Although it has the same concise directions to each place, it also contains more natural and historical information, so people can learn about Pennsylvania's natural heritage without necessarily visiting the places.

But I also hope that the extra information encourages people to visit at least some of the places and experience for themselves the great variety of natural beauty Pennsylvania has to offer.

EASTERN PENNSYLVANIA

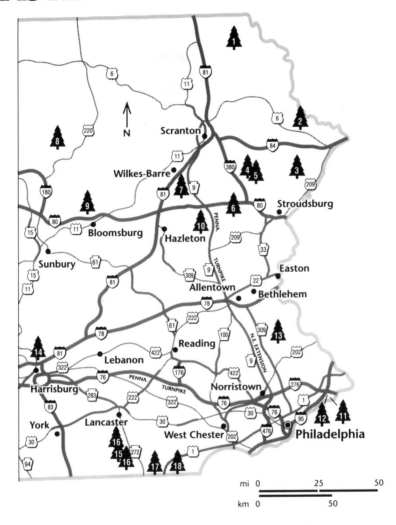

1. FLORENCE SHELLY PRESERVE
2. SHOHOLA FALLS
3. PAINTER SWAMP
4. LEHIGH POND
5. TOBYHANNA STATE PARK
6. LONG POND
7. THE TUBS NATURE AREA
8. KETTLE CREEK GORGE
   WILD AREA
9. JAKEY HOLLOW NATURAL
   AREA
10. LEHIGH GORGE STATE PARK
11. BRISTOL MARSH

12. DELHAAS WOODS
13. QUAKERTOWN SWAMP
14. WILDWOOD LAKE
15. TUCQUAN GLEN /
    PYFER NATURE
    PRESERVES
16. KELLY'S RUN NATURAL AREA
    AND SHENK'S FERRY GLEN
    WILDFLOWER PRESERVE
17. GOAT HILL SERPENTINE
    BARRENS
18. CHROME SERPENTINE BARRENS

1   FLORENCE SHELLY PRESERVE

After years of being drained, bulldozed, or otherwise bludgeoned into "usefulness," wetlands are finally being recognized as the boon they have always been, cradling unique ecosystems that ultimately benefit all of us. The Florence Shelly Preserve in northeastern Susquehanna County is one such example.

Presented as a gift to The Nature Conservancy more than a decade ago by its former owners, Florence and Robert Shelly, the 357-acre preserve contains a 10-acre glacial pond of exceptional purity, a swamp, a boreal bog, and a woodland stream. This diversity of wetland habitats leads to a diversity of plants and animals. As a result, the Florence Shelly Preserve provides a home for between 40 and 60 breeding bird species, 375 vascular plants, and such mammals as otters, mink, beaver, black bears, white-tailed deer, porcupines, coyotes, red squirrels, and woodchucks.

Today the preserve is safeguarded and monitored by a small number of dedicated local residents who have formed the Florence Shelly Stewardship Committee. So far they have developed a mile-and-a-half-long self-guided trail that penetrates a small section of the wetland and is open to the public. They also have a shorter, half-mile trail that includes a boardwalk. For those interested in exploring the area in greater depth, there are several other options.

First, you can join one of the regularly scheduled weekend walks led by members of the committee. Then there are also several specialized walks a year, led by knowledgeable people in such fields as botany and ornithology. Finally, you or a group can make an appointment for a guided walk by calling 717-756-2429 or writing The Nature Conservancy / Florence Shelly Preserve, P.O. Box 157, Thompson, PA 18465.

Members of the Stewardship Committee believe it is vital to educate as many people as possible about the importance of the preserve so they will understand why it should be protected from interference by humans. Their hope is to keep what is there as "seed for the future, . . . like a

Weir's Pond. Florence Shelly Preserve.

Noah's Ark," according to the trail brochure distributed free to those who stop at the glass-enclosed wooden sign to the right of the old road/trail, about 200 feet from the main road.

As you walk along, you will see for yourself the abundant diversity of plants and wildlife the area supports. Along the roadway, dolls' eyes and a vine called virgin's bower are prominent. Other wildflowers to look for include false hellebore and Indian pipes. In the spring you may find such wildflowers as starflower, Indian cucumber-root, Canada mayflower, pink lady's slipper, Solomon's seal, rose-twisted stalk, wood sorrel, goldthread, trout-lily, painted, snow, and purple trilliums, wild ginger, and squirrel corn.

In some areas, the understory of the woods is green with beds of seven species of clubmosses and 15 to 18 species of ferns, including maidenhair, ebony spleenwort, New York, lady, beech, and cinnamon. In the wetter areas are 14 species of the spongy sphagnum moss, while at the outlet of Weir's Pond a rare red algae, *Batrachospermum vagum*, which thrives only in pristine water, grows.

If you take a guided walk in August, as we did, you will find Weir's Pond set amid a haze of purple pickerelweed, its water covered with both white fragrant water-lilies and yellow bullhead-lilies. In spring this glacial pond contains several species of ducks as well as Canada geese, which stop off both at the pond and at the bog area during migration.

There is also beaver activity at the pond's outlet, and in winter members of the Stewardship Committee have found otter slides in the snow. Near the pond in the deep hemlock woods, several enormous tilting rocks are greenly furred with lichens and ferns, which provide a growing medium, in the spring, for nurseries of yellow clintonia.

Weir's Pond is off-limits to the casual visitor, but the old road trail provides at least a glimpse of this unique area. Eventually you reach a woodland stream, with banks lushly covered with cardinal flowers, broad-leaved arrowhead, watercress, and jewelweed. From there, turn right, following the self-guided nature trail along the stream until it makes another right. After passing through a scotch pine area to your right, turn right again until you reach the old road. Then turn left and retrace your steps back to the entrance.

From there, drive another mile north on Pa. Route 171, turn right on Little Ireland Road, and drive a quarter-mile to parking on the right. From there you can take the short trail and boardwalk that lead through a hemlock forest to a view over the beaver-formed Plews or Krall Swamp, depending on what local people you ask. Here you will see abundant bird life every season of the year.

For a better idea of what the Shelly Wetlands contains, I depended on information from enthusiastic members of the Stewardship Committee who told me of nesting wood ducks, eastern bluebirds, and tree swallows, fishing great blue herons, and abundant insect-eating sundews and pitcher plants. In early July purple fringed orchid blooms, but balsam fir, which grows in the swamp area, is green throughout the year.

Like wetlands everywhere, the Florence Shelly Preserve is a place where visitors can find something new and interesting whenever they go there. But then such diversity is the primary virtue of a pristine wetland and one of the reasons why, in an increasingly homogenized society, such refuges for the spirit are needed more than ever.

From Scranton: Take Interstate 81 north 24 miles to Exit 64 (Lenox). Follow Pa. 106 west 0.2 mile to State Highway 92 north. Drive 8.9 miles on 92 north to Gelatt. Then turn right (sign says "Thompson 7" at this easy-to-miss intersection). Proceed 5.8 miles. At the stop sign, turn left on Route 171 north and go 0.6 mile into the center of the town of Thompson. Turn left (north on 171), following the sign to Lanesboro. At precisely 1.3 miles, pull off the highway, park, and walk right to a primitive dirt road through the woods bordered on the left by a field.

There should be a small, yellow nature sanctuary sign posted there. Across High-way 171 is the intersection with Stack Road.

2   SHOHOLA FALLS

If you collect Pennsylvania waterfalls, add Shohola Falls in Pike County to your list. Part of State Game Lands 180, the beauty of the falls has remained intact despite the small dam above it that created 1,150-acre Shohola Lake as a habitat for waterfowl and warm-water fish.

To see migrating waterfowl, visit the area in April. That early in the season, the entrance to the Shohola Recreation Area, just off U.S. Route 6, is still closed, but a portion of the service road around much of the lake is open. Pull into the boat-trailer parking lot overlooking the northern end of Shohola Lake. From there you can easily explore a labyrinth of short interconnecting trails in the recreation area, threading your way through an understory of evergreen sheep laurel as song sparrows and eastern phoebes serenade you.

Usable picnic tables are scattered throughout the woods within easy reach of the restrooms, which are closed for the season. But the trails are not closed, and two lead down both sides of Shohola Falls, each with a different view. The falls tumbles over nine rock ledges into an 80-foot-deep hemlock-enclosed gorge carved by Shohola Creek. The creek itself descends 200 feet in half a mile through a series of falls and rapids, the most spectacular of which is the falls below the dam.

The gorge cliffs, composed of shales and siltstones and dripping with moisture, are the area's best feature. On the east side, the trail follows the base of the cliffs, which gives walkers a close-up view of the mosses and ferns colonizing the rocks. Only evergreen ferns, such as common poly-pody, maidenhair spleenwort, and intermediate woodfern, grow from the rock crevices so early in the season, but a greater variety of ferns and wildflowers colonize the cliffs during the warmer months.

Pockets of soil in the cliffs support small hemlock seedlings, and the roots of two large yellow birches, draped in mosses, snake over the rocks.

View of Shohola Falls.

Fern moss and several species of sphagnum moss soak up the constant spray from Shohola Falls, along with the rubbery liverworts tucked within the mosses. Altogether, this is a place where pteridologists (fern experts) and bryologists (moss experts) could profitably spend some time.

The real reason for visiting Shohola Falls so early in the season, however, is to see migratory waterfowl. Drive along the service road until you reach a permanently gated area just beyond the utility buildings on the left. Pull into the parking lot to the right and walk out to the boat ramp, which will give you a fine vista of the lake. You may be lucky and glimpse a pair of horned grebes, still partially in their black-and-white winter plumage, trying to get airborne. Jaunty male buffleheads bob over the wavelets, their puffy black heads adorned with a large white patch. This makes them one of the easiest of waterfowl to identify.

There may also be male common goldeneyes, which are somewhat similar in coloration to the buffleheads, with a white body, black back, and puffy black-looking head. But a common goldeneye is larger, and close-up its head is actually dark green. In addition, its white head patch is smaller and located between its eye and the base of its bill, instead of being on top of its head and behind its eye like the bufflehead. But paired quacking mallards and honking Canada geese are the most common and noisiest waterfowl species on the lake.

The gated service road makes an excellent hiking trail, and occasionally a path swings off to the right to feeding-plot areas or to the left toward the lake. After walking up the first hill beyond the gate, turn right into a feeding area. Continue ahead until you reach the remnants of a boggy pond dotted with wood-duck nesting boxes. In spring the pond reverberates with the calls of spring peepers. Steeplebush and low-bush blueberry thrive in the spongy sphagnum moss, and mallards seem to consider the area their personal domain.

After returning to the road, descend the hill, and at the bottom, where a stream flows under the road, follow the trail at the left to the lakeshore, watching for a beaver lodge on the right. Creep up to this area for another look at the lake. The lake is four miles long and has many hidden coves, and the service road continues most of the way around it. Depending on time constraints and your stamina, you can continue walking the easy, up-and-down road and investigate the frequent feeding plots and boggy ponds in search of wildlife, as well as scan the lake from different aspects.

In this part of the Poconos where so many lakes are in private hands, Pennsylvanians can be grateful that not only the large lake but also the surrounding 11,372 acres are owned by the Game Commission and open to the public. All you need is a pair of legs or a boat to enjoy Shohola Falls outside of hunting season, which means 52 Sundays of the year and most of the winter, spring, and summer.

From Scranton: Take Interstate 84 east to Exit 9. Proceed north on Pa. 739 0.7 mile to the intersection with Well Road. There is no sign for the road, but an 84 Lumber Company building is on the left, and Lord's Valley Towing is on the right. Follow Well Road 3.8 miles to the intersection with U.S. 6. Turn right and follow Route 6 for 2.1 miles to the main parking area on your right.

3   PAINTER SWAMP

Painter Swamp, in southeastern Pike County, is an idyllic place to watch birds in mid-May. Part of the Delaware State Forest, a portion of both the

View of Painter Swamp.

blue-blazed 28.2-mile Thunder Swamp Trail and the red-blazed 16.7-mile side trails encircle and bisect the 150-acre swamp. But the trails are litter-free, and during our visit we neither saw nor heard another human being. Perhaps that was because it was a weekday and it had been raining hard all morning.

As we pulled into the parking lot, the sun came out and we were greeted by a spring bird chorus at noon—ovenbirds, rose-breasted gros-beaks, wood thrushes, scarlet tanagers, American redstarts, common yel-lowthroats, rufous-sided towhees, black-throated green warblers, and great-crested flycatchers. From that moment on, birds dominated our visit—32 species altogether.

The swamp was really a lake that day, its blue water riffled by the breeze, which kept insects at bay. Four Canada geese honked continually as we slowly circled the upper eastern portion of the swamp, following prominent red blazes. Two wood ducks also flushed from the edge of the swamp. Tree swallows, along with eastern phoebes and blue-gray gnatcatchers, swooped continually over Painter Swamp, snapping up in-sects. In addition to birdsong, the swamp croaked and peeped with frog music.

The trail itself has so much of interest that it is difficult to decide whether to concentrate on the wildflowers at your feet, the birds in the branches, or the several large and interesting tree species. Probably the best of the trees is a good-sized American chestnut with piles of empty chestnut burrs on the ground beneath it, a reminder that at least a few of those wonderful trees are still able to resist the chestnut blight long enough to produce some seeds. The trail also wanders past several large white pines, a magnificent shagbark hickory, and many black spruce trees. Also called "swamp spruce" or "bog spruce," black spruce is a northern tree that extends to the tree limit in northern Canada and Alaska and ranges along the Appalachian Mountains to Virginia. In Pennsylvania it is found mostly in the swamps and bogs of the Poconos.

Woodland wildflowers blooming in mid-May along the trail include the large-flowered bellwort, starflower, sarsaparilla, fringed polygala, Canada mayflower, round-leaved yellow violet, rue anemone, dwarf ging-seng, goldthread, and cut-leaved toothwort. Out in the swamp itself, the bullhead-lilies are in large yellow bud.

But nothing could compete with the sight of yellow warblers foraging against a blue sky, a chestnut-sided warbler searching for insects in a shrub five feet from where I stood, and a Canada warbler, his black "neck-lace" strung across his golden neck and breast, singing what Roger Tory

Peterson calls his "staccato burst, irregularly arranged—chip, chupety swee-ditchety." Denizens of forest undergrowth and shady thickets, nesting Canada warblers have always been particularly abundant in the Poconos. Worm-eating warblers buzzed in the underbrush, while least flycatchers called "che-bec, che-bec." Black-and-white warblers crept along the tree trunks like woodpeckers, singing "weesee, weesee, weesee," and a wood thrush flew up from the ground with its "pip-pip-pip" warning cry.

As we reached the blue-blazed Thunder Swamp Trail leading left toward the Stillwater Natural Area, the air was suddenly filled with unfamiliar birdsong. Because of the volume of sound, I looked for large showy birds, but all I saw were nearly a dozen small brown creepers singing what one writer calls "one of the gems of bird music" as they spiraled up tree trunks. Familiar only with their thin, high-pitched "seee" calls, I found it difficult to connect the rich, full-bodied songs I was hearing with the brown-and-white birds that resemble moving tree bark. Brown creepers commonly sing only on their nesting grounds, and because they prefer mature forests with dead or partly dead trees to supply both food and nesting area (they nest beneath peeling tree bark), Painter Swamp and its environs provide an ideal nesting habitat for the brown creeper.

At this point, halfway along the eastern edge of Painter Swamp, you can either follow the signs left to the Stillwater Natural Area, adding three or six miles to your day, depending on whether you circle the north loop and/or south loop of the natural area, or, for an easier walk, continue straight ahead on the blue-blazed Thunder Swamp Trail as it winds along the lower, eastern side of Painter Swamp. Once you cross the south end, turn right onto a red-blazed trail, which follows above the western end of the swamp and gives excellent overviews of the swamp in several places. From those vantage points we saw more birds—red-eyed vireos, gray catbirds, song sparrows, eastern bluebirds, red-winged blackbirds, American crows, common grackles, blue jays, mallards, and red-tailed hawks.

Altogether, the loop around Painter Swamp is a little more than two miles on almost level terrain, but there is so much to see that it takes several hours. A day spent at Painter Swamp drives home the point that wildlife—including beaver, which have a lodge in the middle of the swamp—is attracted to wetlands. Although we did try another loop that took us through a mile of woods to the north loop of Stillwater Natural Area, once we left the vicinity of the swamp it was difficult to see what few birds there were. But when we returned to the lower end of the swamp, birds were as abundant as ever.

Still, there is no doubt that the 45 miles of trails that wind through this section of the Delaware State Forest are worth exploring. For a copy of the excellent Delaware State Forest Thunder Swamp Trail map, write the Delaware State Forest District Headquarters at 474 Clearview Lane, Stroudsburg, PA 18360, or call 717-424-3001.

From Stroudsburg: Follow Interstate 80 to Exit 52, located between the Delaware River and Stroudsburg. Take U.S. 209 north through a forest of billboards 4 miles to the first traffic light in Marshalls Creek. Turn right on U.S. 209, drive 0.1 mile to the next traffic light, and turn left on Pa. 402 north. In 100 yards, Route 402 bears right with a sign indicating that the highway goes to Resica Falls and Hawley. Drive north into the Poconos along Route 402, 13.9 miles from the traffic light, and turn right onto a paved road marked by a very small sign on the left side of the highway as SR2003. After 1.5 miles, turn left on a narrow gravel road labeled Flat Ridge Road and Silver Lake Road. Proceed 2.1 miles to a parking area on the right marked with signs for Painter Swamp and Thunder Swamp Trail.

4   LEHIGH POND

Lehigh Pond is one of only a few undisturbed and unpolluted bodies of water left in Pennsylvania. Located a few miles northeast of the town of Gouldsboro in Wayne County, this 15-acre glacial kettlehole pond is surrounded by a sphagnum bog and is the focal point of a 3,828-acre northern Poconos wetland recently designated as State Game Lands 312. It is also the headwaters of the Lehigh River, hence its name.

Easily reached by a short scenic trail that winds past huge old hemlock trees and then continues through a tunnel of enormous rhododendron shrubs, the pond itself has a far-north aspect even in mid-May. At that time the deciduous trees in the woodland—red maple, American beech, and yellow birch—are still in flower. In the open boggy area around the pond, tamarack, a deciduous conifer, has barely begun to leaf out. The other prominent conifer tree species—black spruce—grows interspersed with the tamarack.

Tamarack tree in foreground of Lehigh Pond.

Black spruce (*Picea mariana*) is known to invade the edges of cold sphagnum bogs like that surrounding Lehigh Pond. According to naturalist Donald Culross Peattie, "gummers on snowshoes, carrying long poles fitted with chisels to knock off the resinous exudations," used to collect spruce gum for chewing gum. Spruce beer was another product oldtimers made from the trees. Henry David Thoreau claimed the beer "would make [the drinker] see green, and, if he slept, dream that he heard the wind sough among the pines."

The tamarack (*Larix laricina*), also known as "American larch" and "hackmatack," is the only native conifer that sheds its leaves. In late autumn, tamarack needles turn a bright yellow before falling. Throughout the winter months, the tree looks dead, but in the spring clusters of soft, flexible, pale-green needles cover its branches. Tamarack loves the cold and grows as far north as the tree limit. In its southern range, which includes Pennsylvania, it, like the black spruce, is found almost exclusively in cold swamps and sphagnum bogs.

The bog surrounding Lehigh Pond also has an array of interesting shrubs, all of which are members of the Heath family. In May, blueberry shrubs are thickly covered with white bell-shaped blossoms. Sheep laurel and cranberry are still in bud, and so are the bog rosemary and Labrador tea. Any cook who uses rosemary will instantly recognize the spiky leaves of bog rosemary (*Andromeda glaucophylla*). Not only do they look like those of culinary rosemary, a native of the Mediterranean, but they smell like them. A low evergreen shrub with a blue-green cast, bog rosemary grows only in cold bogs, usually in company with pitcher plants and, rarely, in Pennsylvania, with Labrador tea.

Labrador tea (*Ledum groenlandicum*), so named because backwoodsmen once made a potent tea from it, is one of two rare-to-Pennsylvania plants found at Lehigh Pond. It reaches its southern limit in northern Pennsylvania. Like tamarack, it is most common in the far north, ranging up into Greenland, Labrador, and Alaska. For protection from cold, drying winds, the lower surfaces of its thick, leathery evergreen leaves and younger branchlets are covered with a dense woolly coat of hairs.

To reach the edge of Lehigh Pond you should wear rubber boots, because the bog oozes water as you walk. I found one relatively dry spot at the pond's edge where I could sit while my husband photographed pitcher plants. Although the plants don't bloom until June, the pitcher-like heavily veined red or green leaves are easy to spot in the bog.

Pitcher plant (*Sarracenia purpurea*) is cleverly designed to entice insects with its nectar glands and brightly colored veins on its top flap. Once the insects land on the flap, hundreds of downward-pointing hairs on it encourage them to descend into the pitcher but make it almost impossible to climb back out. Slipping and sliding down its smooth vertical sides, the insects accumulate globs of sticky cells from the plant on their feet. They use up their energy in a fight to free themselves and finally give up, falling into the water-filled pitcher, where they drown. The walls of the pitcher also secrete digestive enzymes that eventually absorb the insect tissues. The pitcher plant uses the resultant energy to produce flowers and fruit.

Not all insects succumb to the pitcher plant. Mosquito larvae thrive in the enzyme-rich water; fly larvae feed on the insects that have died there. Some spider species spin their webs across the pitcher's mouth to catch insects on their way in, and tree frogs sit on the leaf rim and snap up passing insects. Altogether, the pitcher plant is not only one of the most attractive of carnivorous plants but also one of the most interesting.

Other plants of interest in the bog are the rare-to-Pennsylvania many-fruited sedge *Carex lasiocarpa* var. *americana,* a herbaceous perennial also known as *Carex filiformis* that likes sphagnum bogs and boggy shores, and the carnivorous sundew.

Despite a spanking breeze during our visit, the cloud of humming black flies was thick. Tree swallows seined the air above the pond for them. Least flycatchers alternately snapped up insects and called "che-bec." A chorus of black-capped chickadees sang their "fee-bee" song, and common yellowthroats called "witchedy, witchedy" from the hidden depths of small shrubs. A northern water snake, head held high, swam to shore beside me and draped itself over a wet log for a few minutes before sliding back down into the water.

Turkey vultures floated past, banking and tilting in the wind. Then suddenly an osprey flapped overhead crying "creer-creer-creer." Ospreys, along with Virginia rails, black and wood ducks, river otters, black bears, beaver, muskrats, and mink, are wetland-related species that thrive in the Lehigh Pond area.

On the walk back through the woods, I heard a host of singing neotropical migrants—ovenbirds, red-eyed vireos, black-throated blue warblers, scarlet tanagers, and rose-breasted grosbeaks. All had access to safe nesting ground in the vast expanse of woods and wetlands that make up SGL 312. In fact, this game land contains two percent of all the wetlands in the Poconos and one half of one percent of all the wetlands in the state.

Best of all, though, is Lehigh Pond, the jewel in the crown. It sparkled pristinely in the clear spring sunlight, a 15,000-year-old body of water that remains as pure as it was when it was first scoured out by a glacier during the Wisconsin Ice Age.

From Interstate 80: Go to Interstate 380. Exit onto Pa. 507. Drive through the town of Gouldsboro. Less than a mile outside town, look for an electrical substation on your right. Look for Game Commission signs on both sides of the road. Go about one mile past the substation and veer off to your left. Cross the Lehigh River (a little stream at this point). Drive a few hundred yards beyond the stream and you'll see a dirt drive on the left with Game Commission signs. Turn in there and park. Take the path to your left.

5   TOBYHANNA STATE PARK

On a beautiful day in mid-May it is difficult to believe that Tobyhanna State Park, located in Monroe and Wayne counties, is part of the heavily touristed Poconos. But that is before the summer season and is the best time to visit, especially if you are interested in observing migrating birds and finding spring wildflowers.

The Yellow Trail, billed by a park handout as "very demanding," has additional precautions, which include "wearing proper footwear," not hiking alone, and being "prepared to 'rock-hop' and cross a few minor wet areas." Actually, it is a relatively easy trail accessible to anyone who likes to walk, although waterproof hiking boots are helpful.

After parking your car in Parking Area 5, begin your walk by following the blue-blazed Lakeside Trail northwest for approximately 1,200 feet and then turning right, still on the Lakeside Trail. When that trail bears off to the left after a short distance, continue straight ahead on the Yellow Trail.

From the moment you leave the car, you will be surrounded by bird-song. Because the tree leaves have barely begun to open, spotting the singers is easy. Knowing birdsongs is also a plus because you can easily distinguish the ovenbirds' piercing "teacher-teacher-teacher" and the rufous-sided towhees' repetitive "drink-your-teas." A short way along the

Bender Swamp along the Yellow Trail. Tobyhanna State Park.

Yellow Trail, there is ideal chestnut-sided warbler habitat, and you should both hear his "sweet, sweet, sweet, I'll switch you" song and see the handsome yellow-crowned warbler with chestnut sides separating his white breast from his yellow-and-black wings and back.

Other birds that fill the woods with music include scarlet tanagers, rose-breasted grosbeaks, red-eyed vireos, and worm-eating warblers. Scarlet tanager males with their blood-red bodies and black wings, and the females with golden breasts and green backs, are easy to see. So are the thick-billed, black-and-white male rose-breasted grosbeaks sporting a showy triangle of rose-red on their breasts, although the females have inconspicuously streaked brown-and-white bodies. While rose-breasted grosbeaks sing like "robins who have taken voice lessons," according to ornithologist/artist Roger Tory Peterson, scarlet tanagers sound like "robins with a sore throat."

In direct contrast to those brilliantly colored birds are what birdwatchers call, with sinking hearts, the Empidonax flycatchers—five look-alike species with light eye rings, two small, whitish wingbars, and overall greenish-gray backs with whitish breasts. These species are best distinguished by voice, habitat, and way of nesting and are known as least, alder, willow, yellow-bellied, and Acadian flycatchers. The day I visited the park, a portion of the Yellow Trail rang with the "che-bec" call-song of the least flycatcher. For a few minutes it sounded as if all the least flycatchers in the world had gathered for a conference.

Birds are only part of the natural spectacle that makes covering miles a difficult prospect. The bell-shaped blossoms of high-bush blueberries are in full bloom and a reminder that this area of Pennsylvania is renowned for its large black bear population. Judging from the number of blossoms, the area should be loaded with bear food in July. At the stream crossing over the black tannin water of Tobyhanna Creek, starflowers, Canada mayflowers, and false hellebore grow in the spongy sphagnum moss.

Both before and after the stream crossing, portions of the woods floor are blanketed with painted trillium. Painted trillium (*Trillium undulatum*), its three white petals marked with a red blaze in the center, is the loveliest of the trilliums. Unlike the four other eastern North American trilliums, the painted trillium likes bogs and acidic woods and is often found under hemlock trees. Those along the Yellow Trail, however, are growing mostly beneath the predominately American beech, sugar and red maple, and yellow birch forest of mature northern hardwoods that lines the trail, along with a thin scattering of hemlocks.

The Yellow Trail cuts through Bender Swamp, the largest wetland of an area filled with wetlands, but it is not soggy. Instead, you only glimpse the swamp through the forest until about a quarter-mile beyond the powerline right-of-way, where the trail suddenly veers to the left. To obtain a better view of the famed wetlands of Tobyhanna and nearby Gouldsboro state parks—what Kimball Erdman and Paul Weigman, in their *Preliminary List of Natural Areas in Pennsylvania*, call "the finest collection of wetlands in the state park system"—plunge straight ahead to the edges of an open bog surrounded by black spruce and northern larch trees. Filled with high-bush blueberry shrubs, the area rings with the songs and calls of black-capped chickadees and blue jays. During my visit, I faintly heard the ethereal song of a wood thrush, and a nearby shrub held a Canada warbler, a black-throated blue warbler, and a black-and-white warbler, all feeding on insects and oblivious to my close presence. On the wet ground, patches of goldthread bloom, another lover of bogs, mountains, and cool northern woods.

At that point, you will have covered only half of the 2.75-mile-long Yellow Trail, so you can either finish the trail and retrace your steps, or turn back and follow an even easier path with a different aspect—the five-mile circular trail around Tobyhanna Lake. This hardened base trail is designed for biking and hiking in the summer, and for cross-country skiing and snowmobiling in the winter and is even wheelchair accessible.

You can either pick up the Lakeside Trail from where it branches off the Yellow Trail and take the entire loop, or return to your car and drive back over the dam, pulling off to a parking area on the right. This southwestern end of the lake seems more like a wetland, and indeed great blue herons frequent the shallow water. Views of the lakeshore framed with white birch trees highlight this portion of the trail. Here too birds sing and wildflowers bloom. It is, however, far more heavily used than the Yellow Trail, and voices ring out from people fishing, boating, picnicking, and generally enjoying the lake area. That is quite a contrast to the deserted Yellow Trail, where the only sounds you hear are those of singing birds. On that trail, you get a glimpse of the 2,000-foot-high Pocono Plateau as it might have looked centuries ago.

From Stroudsburg: Follow Interstate 80 west 15 miles, then Interstate 380 west toward Scranton. After 7.1 miles, get off at Exit 7 (Pa. 423) and turn right, following signs for Tobyhanna State Park. At 0.3 mile, stop for U.S. 611, then proceed straight ahead 0.3 mile farther. Turn left at the stop sign, following 423 into the community of Tobyhanna. After 0.1 mile, turn right on 423 toward the park. Proceed 1.6 miles to the parking area on the left for Lakeside Trail. To reach Parking Area 5, drive 0.8 mile farther on Route 423. Turn left into a park road, pass the park office on your right, and continue 0.6 mile to the parking area on the right.

6   LONG POND

Long Pond, in the Poconos, consists of a 2,000-acre wetland surrounded by a 5,600-acre pitch pine/scrub oak barren. Because the area contains 32 rare-to-Pennsylvania plant and animal species, the Eastern Pennsylvania Chapter of The Nature Conservancy is trying to preserve as much of the site as possible for future generations to enjoy. Already they have purchased 400 acres, and other portions, owned by the City of Bethlehem Water Authority, are also open to the public. However, much of this western Monroe County site remains in private hands that often see such

Tunkhannock Stream outlet from Long Pond.

"wasteland" as useful only if it is drained, developed, or quarried. Such has been the fate of most of the once-numerous barren ecosystems in the northeastern United States.

The Long Pond barrens are only a small portion of what is called the Pocono glacial till barrens—a large expanse of pitch pine and dwarf scrub oak forests interspersed with moorlike heathlands, swamps, bogs, and marshes. In fact, according to the Pennsylvania Natural Diversity Inventory, the Pocono glacial till barrens appear to be the only natural community of its kind in the world. Because of its rarity, scientists do not yet understand how it functions.

To make some sense of the system, The Nature Conservancy has launched an in-depth study and discovered, by using a computerized geographic information system (GIS), that 50 years ago the Pocono barrens were more than twice as large. While some of the decline appears to be due to the suppression of naturally occurring fire, which once kept the barrens open, most of it is directly attributable to residential developments that have penetrated into nearly one-third of the remaining area inhabited by barrens vegetation.

Luckily a portion of the Long Pond barrens has remained much as botanist Frederick Pursh described it during a botanical excursion he made there in 1807. After relatively unexciting plant-hunting in the Delaware Water Gap, he was elated to discover an entirely different plant community ". . . coming to the barrens, in the top," where he "soon found Cornus Canadensis" (bunchberry). "This mountain [Pokono, as he called it] seems to be a good deal higher than the blue ridge [Blue Mountain] and its vegetable production shows the relation of its climate with that of Canada," he wrote on June 15, 1807. Pursh was particularly interested in the rhodora, which "grows here in great plenty," and in the "Kalmia angustifolia" (sheep laurel), a plant "natural to these grounds, either wet or dry."

Today in late May, a visitor to the Long Pond barrens can still see vast expanses of pink-blossoming rhodora, a waist-high shrub of the Heath family immortalized by Ralph Waldo Emerson:

> Rhodora! If the sages ask thee why
> This charm is wasted on the earth and sky,
> Tell them, dear, if eyes were made for seeing
> Then Beauty is its own excuse for being.

Rhodora is a northern shrub that grows no farther south than northeastern Pennsylvania and that extends through New England, Quebec, and Newfoundland. Of all the known remaining barrens in the northeastern United States, only the Long Pond barrens boasts rhodora as its dominant shrub.

The closely related sheep laurel, with its crimson-pink flowers growing in the center of its leaf clusters, is also a common understory Heath shrub at the Long Pond barrens. In fact, it is the Heath family's predominance there that makes the site so rich in rare moth species. So far, 15 rare moths have been discovered in the barrens, including the Amianthium-borer moth. The larvae of this moth have developed an immunity to the highly toxic bulb of fly-poison (*Amianthium muscaetoxicum*), which they bore into and feed on before pupating. Although fly-poison is a fairly common wildflower in sandy woods and the coastal plains from Long Island and Pennsylvania to the south, the Amianthium-borer moth has been found in only two other sites in the world!

And so it goes for most of the other rare plants and animals of the area. Six of the 15 moths have been found in Pennsylvania only at the Long Pond barrens, and several more at only one additional site, including *Zale curema*, which feeds on pitch pine. A sixteenth rare moth—the sundew moth—is associated with the wetlands, and again that is the only place in the state it is known to live.

While most of us will never see the moth population of the barrens, it is possible to find some rare plants—Hartford fern, creeping snowberry shrub, both blunt manna-grass and fall dropseed muhly grass, and the variable sedge (*Carex polymorpha*)—known from only nine other sites worldwide. Six additional rare plants and two dragonfly species live in the wetland areas.

To get an overview of both the barrens and the wetlands, first stop at the Tunkhannock Stream outlet from Long Pond. Here grow such rare-to-Pennsylvania shrubs as the sweet bayberry and Labrador tea, as well as the more common leatherleaf and meadowsweet. All are indicative of a northern boreal wetland. At the wetlands' edges, a forest of hemlock, red spruce, and tamarack predominate. It is possible to put a canoe into the water at that point and explore the wetlands, but if you prefer to walk, proceed by car 2.4 miles to a T-intersection and turn right. After 1.4 more miles, bear left and drive another 1.4 miles to a gated entrance on the left. This is the Grass Lake area owned by the Bethlehem Watershed Authority.

Park near the gate and walk down the path to observe the abundant rhodora, sheep laurel, and fly-poison. Rufous-sided towhees scratch in the underbrush, and prairie warblers call from the shrubs. A large deer stood like a signpost at the fork in the path that marked our right turn when we visited in late May. Then we followed a chorus of spring peepers and American toads that led us, after 200 or so yards, to a left turn into the area surrounding remote Grass Lake. Two great blue herons lifted off the water to the accompaniment of a drumming ruffed grouse and buzzing red-winged blackbirds.

After absorbing the far-north feel of this wild area, return to your car and continue along the dirt road another half-mile to a second pull-off on the left, where you can see part of the Long Pond barren.

Even in May you need a broad-brimmed hat and sunblock to prevent a bad sunburn, because the predominant low-growing scrub oaks are broken only occasionally by a taller pitch pine or gray birch tree. For the most part, you will feel like Gulliver in the Land of the Lilliputians, taller than most of the vegetation surrounding you. That makes birdwatching easier, especially during the warbler migration, because the birds—for instance, chestnut-sided and Nashville warblers—are forced to land on branches at eye level.

This area too is owned by the Bethlehem Watershed Authority, and we chose the shorter of two possible unmarked circular trails. Walk straight up the trail to the first left turn, and follow that until it reaches the dirt road you drove in on. Then take a left back to your car for an easy one-mile walk on level ground.

Finally, to see the area owned by The Nature Conservancy, return 1.9 miles the way you came and bear left. After another 1.9 miles, at the intersection with Route 115, turn right. Drive 1.9 miles farther and pull off at a gated dirt road on the right. This land has a greater diversity of taller trees and also contains the rare variable sedge. You can walk straight in as far as you want to, but you will probably be stopped eventually by wet feet because the barrens meld into the wetlands. When you return to your car, continue 4.7 miles more on Route 115 and you will be back at Exit 43 of Interstate 80, having completed, by car and on foot, a circle tour of Long Pond.

To see the barrens at its best, when it is pink with rhodora, visit in mid-May before it gets too hot. The wetland is more interesting in the summer when both of the rare dragonflies—the elegant skimmer and spotted blue darner—zoom over the backwaters of Long Pond. If you are lucky, you might also see a river otter or a black bear, both residents of the wetland.

The Nature Conservancy's barrens research program has already begun in-depth plant censuses in connection with planned ecological burning experiments. It has also discovered that the entire Pocono barrens does not occur, as once thought, on a rare geological formation, the largest remaining deposit of 140,000-year-old Illinoian glacial till in the East. Instead, a large area of barrens is on the more common and only 10,000-year-old Wisconsinian glacial till.

Another interesting discovery, concerning the hydrogeology of the Long Pond watershed, is that stream channels, deeply buried by glacial rubble for more than 140,000 years, still serve as important conduits for groundwater flow. It is therefore important that this rare system be thoroughly studied and understood before land-use changes are made. With this information, The Nature Conservancy hopes it will be able to identify the most important tracts and protect them. All of us will greatly benefit from their farsighted planning, because it should make it possible for our children and grandchildren to see in the year 2007 what Frederick Pursch saw back in 1807.

From Interstate 80: Take Exit 43 (Pa. 115). Turn south on Route 115 toward Effort. After 3.1 miles, bear left toward the Long Pond and Pocono Raceway sign. Drive another 1.5 miles, then pull in at the right to view Tunkhannock Stream outlet from Long Pond.

7   THE TUBS
NATURE AREA

In 1975 a small group of concerned citizens in northeastern Pennsylvania, along with Wilkes College professors and students, formed The Tubs Committee. They wanted to save a unique natural area four miles southeast of downtown Wilkes-Barre in Luzerne County. Known locally as The Tubs or Whirlpool Canyon, its primary attraction is a series of seven large "potholes," or "tubs," gouged out of the underlying bedrock by the continuous flow of the short (1.2-mile-long) but powerful Wheelbarrow Run.

To read a brief history of The Tubs project is to be impressed by the incredible determination of the many citizens who volunteered their time and expertise to preserve The Tubs Nature Area. After obtaining a series of county, state, and federal grants that funded land acquisitions and minimal development to form a county-owned park, the 532-acre site was formally opened to the public on July 8, 1992.

Today the casual visitor would find it difficult to believe that the newly paved access road once enabled people to dump tons of trash on the site. Beginning in 1983, volunteers representing local, civic, and environmental organizations started to hold periodic cleanups. In 1986 a mammoth effort on the part of 100 volunteers removed 11 dumptruck loads of debris, and 7 pickup truck loads of garbage, including an abandoned car. The road was then gated and the area was periodically patrolled by park employees, a process that continues today. Volunteers still donate their time to keep the site tidy.

Consequently, The Tubs Nature Area is no longer a local hangout and dump site but a source of community pride. And no wonder. The care and planning that has gone into both preserving the area and making the place accessible to all is evident. A short walk from the main parking lot takes the visitor along a wheelchair-accessible paved trail where Wheelbarrow Run joins Laurel Run and offers a beautiful view upstream.

For the minimally agile, the 0.4-mile Tubs Trail, marked with red blazes, is a fine introduction to the nature area. Turn left at the North

Closeup of a tub. The Tubs Nature Area.

Footbridge and climb upward through the narrow, steep-walled ravine on the right and the barrens-like scrubland on the left. The scrubland vegetation is a result of human-set, periodic fires that have swept over the area. Scrub or bear oak and pitch pine, two of the dominant tree species, thrive in dry, open, infertile areas.

Pitch pine, also called hard, jack, black, or yellow pine, is fire-resistant and often the only tree species that can survive on land that has been repeatedly burned over. It is easily identified because it is the only native pine species that has needles in bundles of three. In addition, it has ovoid-shaped cones and reddish-brown, deeply fissured bark.

Scrub oak germinates quickly after forest fires, and with its short trunk and stiff, contorted branches it quickly forms a dense protective cover for wildlife. In addition it bears small acorns that provide food for wild turkey, ruffed grouse, white-tailed deer, and small rodents.

The shrubs in this area also indicate barren lands with sterile and acid soils: sheep laurel with its deep rose-purple blossoms, the larger, white-blossomed mountain laurel, and the low-bush blueberry, which bears white or pink bell-shaped flowers. Bracken fern, wintergreen (also known as teaberry), and trailing arbutus are the dominant ground covers.

In contrast, the moist ravine along Wheelbarrow Run is deeply shaded by eastern hemlock, red maple, and black birch trees. Large-leaved mountain holly grows in the understory. Some of the more common deep-woods wildflowers are Indian cucumber-root, Canada mayflower, pink lady's slipper, whorled aster, jack-in-the-pulpit, and Indian pipe.

The east side of the ravine is quite steep, but a ship's ladder has been permanently affixed to the rocks so walkers can safely and easily descend. Then the ravine widens as it continues to the South Footbridge, which had to be brought in on pulleys and is constructed of tough, indestructible eekke wood from Africa.

The western side of the trail leads through a dense forest of hemlock and black birch, and then into a zone of tall pitch pine and maturing oak. Another cool, moist woods wildflower grows in scattered patches—the bunchberry or dwarf cornel, a member of the Dogwood family. Like dogwood flowers, the flowers of bunchberry are actually the center cluster of insignificant greenish blossoms and not the large, showy, white (or pinkish) petal-like bracts. That flower grows on a slender peduncle or stalk an inch or more above the distinctive whorl of six leaves. The plant is even more obvious in late August, when it bears its fruit of tightly clustered scarlet berries.

This section of the trail affords the best views of the "potholes." Scientists differ over how those potholes were formed. At first it was thought that they had been etched by glacial meltwater during the Pleistocene epoch 10,000 years ago. According to Alan R. Geyer and William H. Bolles, in *Outstanding Scenic Geological Features of Pennsylvania*, geologists theorized that "when a meltwater stream flowing through the glacier plunged over the front edge of the ice, or over an ice cliff within the glacier, the volume of meltwater, hydrostatic pressure, and abrasive action of rock fragments etched tub-like potholes up to 30 feet across and 20 feet deep in the sandstone and conglomerate of the Pocono Formation. . . . [Then] as the glacier receded, a series of seven potholes and a gorge were left exposed."

The latest theory, by Bloomsburg University professor Duane D. Braun, disputes this. Braun believes that the potholes were formed by Wheelbarrow Run after the glacier retreated. Whatever the truth of the matter, the result is a natural phenomenon of impressive beauty that is rightly the central focus of The Tubs Nature Area.

Once visitors finish the Tubs Trail, they can turn left and follow Laurel Run upstream along the blue-blazed Audubon Trail, a longer, 1.5-mile loop that is named in recognition of the trail work being done by the Greater Wyoming Valley chapter of the National Audubon Society.

The roar of Wheelbarrow Run makes it difficult to hear bird songs, but some of the more obvious species are black-capped chickadees, rufous-sided towhees, ovenbirds, wood thrushes, ruby-throated hummingbirds (probably attracted by the scarlet blossoms of the cardinal flowers that grow on the banks of Laurel Run), black-billed and yellow-billed cuckoos, and several woodpecker and warbler species.

The usual mammal species for wild Pennsylvania are also present— black bears, white-tailed deer, red and gray squirrels, chipmunks, raccoons, beaver, woodchucks, and skunks, as well as snowshoe hares.

All in all, you can spend many enjoyable hours walking the expanding trail system at The Tubs Nature Area in search of wild plants and animals. But you will probably be impressed most by the geologic forces that carved those seven tubs and agree with the naturalist/writer Henry David Thoreau, who once wrote: "The finest workers in stone are not copper or steel tools, but the gentle touches of air and water working at their leisure with a liberal allowance of time."

From Wilkes-Barre: Follow Pa. 115 east out of the valley. Proceed 1.6 miles beyond the intersection with Interstate 81 and make a very sharp right turn onto the

entrance road for the Tubs Nature Area, which is marked by a sign. Parking is
0.2 mile down the hill on the left.

8   KETTLE CREEK GORGE WILD AREA

On a sparkling day in late October, a visit to the 2,600-acre Kettle Creek
Gorge Wild Area in Sullivan County will have all the ingredients of a
wilderness experience. Remote and ruggedly beautiful, the wild area has
two spectacular waterfalls along Falls Run, and another on Kettle Creek
itself, which is also a wilderness trout stream. Part of the Wyoming State
Forest, this recently designated wild area also includes the 774-acre Kettle
Creek Gorge Natural Area.

The 59-mile Loyalsock Trail provides excellent access into the wild area.
After parking in the pull-off on the left side of Brunnerdale Road, follow
the double yellow blazes of the Loyalsock Trail northwest along Ogdonia
Run, and be prepared to rock-hop over numerous stream crossings.
Golden-crowned kinglets forage in the hemlocks along the stream and
have probably migrated to the area for the winter. Although more and
more golden-crowned kinglets are nesting in Pennsylvania, they prefer
to build their nests high in spruce trees, either in native black spruce in
the boggy areas of the Poconos, or in mature plantations of Norway
spruce. So in most areas of the commonwealth, they remain one of the
most attractive of fall and winter bird visitors and can usually be found
associating with black-capped chickadees, downy woodpeckers, tufted
titmice, and brown creepers.

Turn right (northeast), still on the Loyalsock Trail, and follow Falls Run
until you reach Angel Falls, which you can glimpse through the mostly
leafless hardwoods several hundred feet away. Along the trail, look for
New York, Christmas, and common polypody ferns, the last lingering
blossoms of blue-stemmed goldenrod, and the leaves of wood sorrel. The
understory birches, still retaining most of their leaves, which have turned
gold and beige, glow in the light of a radiant October day.

Angel Falls. Kettle Creek Gorge Wild Area.

Before you reach Angel Falls, the trail is steep and must be carefully negotiated, but it is worth climbing for the view of the falls, which tumble over ledgy rock in three separate streams. After spending plenty of time appreciating the setting, climb up above Angel Falls, still on the Loyalsock Trail, but where it bears left take the unmarked side trail to the right. After a few hundred feet, this trail leads to a second falls, which is guarded by a giant hemlock tree. That unnamed falls drops straight off the mountainside and is framed, in autumn, by the gold and red leaves of red maple saplings. Jack-in-the-pulpit, bearing clumps of scarlet berries, grows in among the rocks near the falls.

Retrace your steps back to Loyalsock Trail and continue a steep and rocky climb to the top at 1,972 feet, a rise of nearly 700 feet from Brunnerdale Road. This area has numerous American beech trees surrounded by clumps of the still-blooming, parasitic beechdrops, which feed directly on beech tree roots. Fleshy-tan in color, they blend in well with the understory, so if you don't know what you are looking at you might mistake them for tree sprouts. Beds of three kinds of clubmosses—shining, ground cedar, and staghorn—blanket the forest floor. Wild black cherry, cucumber magnolia, and tulip trees are abundant. A sparse scattering of leaves still cling to their branches, imparting the last subtle colors of autumn to the woods. Hairy woodpeckers and white-breasted nuthatches call loudly while they forage on the tree trunks.

Still following the Loyalsock Trail, descend nearly 500 feet into the quiet bowl of the Kettle Creek Gorge Natural Area, a heavily forested deep ravine with second-growth hardwoods, aspen, and several species of oak trees. As you continue descending, keep an eye out for a sign with a blue X that points off to the left and after a few hundred feet leads to deeply creviced boulders. From those boulders you will have a spectacular vista of the Kettle Creek Gorge. Retrace your steps back to the Loyalsock Trail and continue your descent down to Kettle Creek.

Once you reach the creek, you must take the precarious two-log crossing over rushing water. Then continue upstream (right), still on the Loyalsock Trail. When you hear what sounds like a waterfall, bushwack back down to the stream for a view of a low, ledgy waterfall with one polished, almost-round rock sticking up on its left side and a small cavern on its right. The leaves of the spring-blooming foamflower still remain in the flat areas beside the stream.

Resume following the Loyalsock Trail upstream. When the trail reaches McCarty Road, continue right, still paralleling Kettle Creek on the Loyalsock Trail, which now follows McCarty Road. It was in this area that we played hide-and-seek with a migrating American woodcock that kept flushing in the wet areas above the trail.

After 0.3 mile, McCarty Road fords the stream. You have the choice of rock-hopping, wading, or going about a quarter of a mile upstream, as I did, until you find a fallen tree to inch across. Loyalsock Trail bears off left in this area, but continue straight ahead on McCarty Road for just over a mile, climbing 700 feet to the top of the mountain. Ignore the right turn and bear left on McCarty Road through the edge of a recently lumbered area in which all the hemlocks were left.

After two and a half miles on McCarty Road you reach Brunnerdale Road. Turn right and follow the road a short way until you reach the parking area. Altogether this circuit is 6.4 miles, with about 1,400 feet of vertical climbing. You should be in reasonable shape and take along a trail lunch and water so you can spend a leisurely day. Also, wear good hiking boots and be prepared to wade, rock-hop, or log-cross cold, rushing mountain streams.

The Loyalsock Trail is known for its rugged character, and certainly this section through Kettle Creek Gorge Wild Area lives up to that reputation. But it is worth the effort to enjoy one of the most beautiful and tranquil places in the commonwealth.

From Williamsport: Follow Interstate 180 east (U.S. 220 north) for 5.3 miles to the exit for Pa. 87, Montoursville. Follow Route 87 north 20.4 miles and turn right on a gravel road (Ogdonia Road). The intersection is marked by a sign for the Camp Lycogis parking area, which is next to the turnoff. Follow Ogdonia Road 2.9 miles and take a left fork onto Brunnerdale Road. The parking area is 0.3 mile farther on the left.

9   JAKEY HOLLOW NATURAL AREA

Tucked down between two cornfields, the 59-acre Jakey Hollow Natural Area is a remnant of primeval forest in Columbia County. Located along

Exposed tree roots along stream. Jakey Hollow Natural Area.

a small tributary of Little Fishing Creek five miles north of Bloomsburg, it was purchased by the Pennsylvania Bureau of Forests in 1990 specifically as a natural area.

Many years ago, the two Crawford brothers walked through Jakey Hollow on their way to school. Even then they recognized it as a special place, and when the land came up for sale in the 1950s the brothers outbid a lumber company for it and protected the area. Finally, Ward Crawford sold it to the Pennsylvania Bureau of Forests. The upper half of the hollow, which has never been logged, is covered with virgin hemlock, white pine, and hardwoods. An excellent mixed stand of second-growth oak, hemlock, and hardwoods grows in the lower half of the hollow.

Although today it is officially part of the Wyoming State Forest, most of which is in western Sullivan County, Jakey Hollow Natural Area is a lone outpost in Columbia County, surrounded by cleared private land. When we visited the area, the crash of machinery from a nearby stone quarry assaulted our ears as soon as we emerged from our car. But once we began the gentle 100-foot descent into Jakey Hollow, the quarry noise faded. It was as if we had stepped back into preindustrial America when natural sounds predominated.

The well-defined path leads visitors into the upper half of the hollow, which contains the virgin hemlock, white pine, and hardwoods, such as the giant American beech tree scarred with the usual human carvings. At the base of the trail, turn right and follow the footpath upstream. This is definitely a place for wanderers, not hikers, since the area is small and confined. The trails are faint and often blocked by trees, left lying where they fell so they could return all their nutrients to the soil and serve as nurse trees for wildflowers, ferns, and new trees. On one rotting log covered with fern moss, mitrewort (bishop's cap) blossomed, while black birch saplings were nurtured on another fallen tree.

Skunk cabbage, dwarf ginseng, and trout-lilies carpeted the wet areas along the stream. Other spring wildflowers included Indian cucumber-root, both Solomon's seal and false Solomon's seal, Canada mayflowers, mayapples, wild geranium, sweet white violets, and kidneyleaf buttercups. The buttercups (*Ranunculus abortivus*) have tiny, inconspicuous yellow flowers that don't look much like the usual meadow buttercups, so it is best to identify them by their kidney-shaped basal leaves.

On the misty, moist day of our visit, tender new leaves of jewelweed and black cohosh had emerged from the soil. Black cohosh (*Cimicifuga racemosa*), a three-to-eight-foot-tall, leafy-stemmed woodland plant, has long terminal racemes of feathery white flowers that bloom in the summer. Also called "bugbane," its flowers, which have a disagreeable scent, were used in rural homes to drive away flies and bugs. Because the Indians believed the thick knotty root of the plant was a cure for snakebites, it was also known as "black snakeroot." Other medicinal uses over the years have been as a treatment for rheumatism, dropsy, and nervous diseases. Whether it is a curative or not, still another alternate name, "fairy candles," seems to best describe the beauty of its wandlike flowers, which "shoot up in the shadowy woods of midsummer like so many ghosts," in the words of Mrs. William Starr Dana's little classic *How to Know the Wild Flowers*.

Jakey Hollow Natural Area also supports many fern species, such as evergreen wood, lady, cinnamon, sensitive, and Christmas ferns, which grow in a ground cover of shining clubmoss and partridgeberry. In other words, the usual native plants flourish in Jakey Hollow.

The birds too are typical woodland species, a mixture of singing neotropical migrants, such as rose-breasted grosbeaks, scarlet tanagers, blue-gray gnatcatchers, solitary vireos, ovenbirds, and worm-eating warblers, and resident birds: black-capped chickadees, northern cardinals, and tufted titmice.

But the dominant birds were blue jays, whose cacophony of calls and songs that sound like wind chimes echoed through Jakey Hollow. American crows and brown-headed cowbirds were also plentiful. All three species inhabit what ecologist Larry Harris calls "the fragmented forest" in his book of the same title, and they are all detrimental to the nesting success of neotropical migrants. Brown-headed cowbirds lay their eggs in the unsuspecting migrants' nests. The resultant cowbird nestlings, which are bigger and pushier than the migrants' offspring, dominate the food, mature faster, and often are the only youngsters that survive to fledgling status. Once a relatively rare grassland species, their numbers exploded and they increased their geographical range after the large forests were cleared and transformed into farmland.

Blue jays, once deep-forest birds, have adjusted to small woodlots, where it is easier to find the nests of other birds and eat both their eggs and nestlings. American crows are open-country birds and benefited from the settlement and farming of Pennsylvania, particularly the cornfields. They, like the blue jays, eat the eggs and nestlings of songbirds.

Small patches of forest like Jakey Hollow Natural Area are also more vulnerable to mammalian predators such as raccoons and opossums, which do not like large tracts of unbroken forest. So while Jakey Hollow looks and sounds like a primary forest should, the success rate of nesting birds there is probably low.

For those reasons, preserving small patches of primary forest is not enough to save vulnerable and increasingly rare bird species that thrive only in large tracts of unbroken forest. Land managers now hope to link such remnant areas to larger tracts, to keep so-called "edge predators" from decimating deep-forest species. If the areas are large enough, they should enable a greater diversity of bird species to reproduce successfully.

Nevertheless, Jakey Hollow Natural Area, despite its size, is a wild, green sample of pre-European settlement Pennsylvania forests. Because two private citizens cared enough to save Jakey Hollow instead of log it, citizens of the commonwealth have a refuge for the spirit and a place to spend quiet hours in the company of giant trees, flowing water, singing birds, and blossoming wildflowers.

From Interstate 80: Take Exit 34, the Bloomsburg/Buckhorn Exit, follow Pa. 42 north toward Millville. After 1.0 mile, turn left at the stop sign, still following Route 42 north. Proceed 2.2 miles from the stop sign and turn right onto a narrow road. Across the highway, a sign announces "HRI Inc., Columbia Asphalt Divi-

sion." Immediately after the right turn, the road crosses a narrow concrete bridge over Little Fishing Creek and bears to the right. About 200 feet beyond the bridge, make a very sharp left turn onto a dirt road that climbs up the hill. (Sign indicates no winter maintenance.) Follow the dirt road 0.4 mile and watch for the signs in the woods on the left, not easily visible from the road, that announce Jakey Hollow Natural Area and mark the trail down into the hollow.

10   LEHIGH GORGE
STATE PARK

To whitewater boaters, Lehigh Gorge State Park in Carbon and Luzerne counties is the place to go when the water in the Lehigh River is high. The heaviest use of this as yet undeveloped and incomplete state park is by rafters and the five concessionaires who supply a variety of tours for them. Because the river drops 735 feet in 33 miles, this small but turbulent watercourse offers continuous Class II and Class III rapids—relatively safe, but exciting.

There is also an abandoned railroad-bed trail stretching 30 miles from White Haven to Jim Thorpe that provides scenic, easy walking and bicycling for those who prefer to stay on dry land. Above White Haven to the park's terminus at Francis E. Walter Dam, the river has been stocked with trout, so it is along this six-mile stretch of trail-less area that fishermen and women congregate for a wilderness fishing experience.

Because no camping is permitted in the park, it is difficult for a walker to see the entire gorge in one day, and many bicyclists would be hard-pressed unless they had a vehicle parked at either end of the trail. But if you enjoy walking on a level surface over scenic terrain—which includes three picturesque waterfalls, several stretches of white water, and a host of birds and wildflowers—your best bet is to head for the park office at the village of Rockport.

During rafting weekends in spring, fall, and whenever water is released at the dam upriver, you must park in the lot outside the office and walk down the narrow road to the trail, because the lot at the trailhead

Lehigh River near Rockport. Lehigh Gorge State Park.

is only for white-water concessionaires and their large buses.

Once you reach the trail, turn left over the bridge and through the gated area. After less than half a mile you will come to Buttermilk Falls, a lovely waterfall that tumbles down over huge rocks. Retrace your steps back to the Rockport access point, paying particular attention, in the spring, to the pockets of soil in the rock cliffs beside the trail. Each supports a miniature hanging garden of wildflowers, including false Solomon's seal, several species of yellow and purple violets, and butter-and-eggs. Best of all are the nodding red bells of wild columbine (*Aquilegia canadensis*), fragile-looking wildflowers of the buttercup family that have a special affinity for rock crevices, although they also grow in rocky woods from Manitoba to Quebec and as far south as Georgia. Because of their long flower tubes and red color, they are pollinated principally by ruby-throated humming-birds, which seem to synchronize their migration northward with the blooming of wild columbine.

Downstream from Rockport, both the exposure and the vegetation changes. The north-facing slope is covered by enormous rhododendron shrubs growing beneath a dense canopy of hemlock trees. But the rocks persist and so do the waterfalls, the first an unnamed falls a half-mile south of Rockport. This falls is narrower than Buttermilk Falls. Shrubs and small trees frame its edges, most notably shadbush and hobblebush. The presence of the latter is encouraging, because this northern member of the viburnum family, with its distinctive heart-shaped leaves, is favorite deer browse and so has been eliminated in more accessible Pennsylvania locales. In fact, although the park is open to hunting, both the hunted and the hunter would have a difficult time climbing up and down the gorge slopes, which can be 1,000 feet high in some places.

That, of course, is part of the charm of this long, narrow, 5,900-acre park. Despite its location in a heavily populated area of the state, its steep walls close out both the sights and the sounds of the outside world. Except for the intense greenery of late spring and summer, it could be a remote canyon in the West. To create that illusion, the state always adds an additional 100-foot buffer strip beyond both rims of the gorge whenever it is able to purchase additional tracts of land for the park. On the east side of the gorge, beyond the park boundaries, the land from one end of the park to the other is owned either by the Game Commission (State Game Lands 141 and 40) or by the Department of Environmental Resources (Hickory Run State Park).

The area to the right of the trail remains dense and dark, and all you can do is listen to the songs of deep-woods bird species, such as the ovenbird, scarlet tanager, and rose-breasted grosbeak. Because the extreme ruggedness of the gorge prevented logging on the steepest slopes, the largest stands of virgin timber in eastern Pennsylvania are found here. But the river side of the trail is framed with smaller trees, making it easier to watch foraging Nashville warblers on a May day, or to look overhead at the turkey vultures wheeling above the river.

The third waterfall is about a mile and a half beyond the second one and is an excellent place to stop and eat a bag lunch. If you take frequent side trips down to the river's edge to watch the white-water rafters or simply to get a view, you will not cover a lot of ground in a day, but you will feel as if you have retreated from the world for a time.

Because Lehigh Gorge State Park is one of the least developed of all our state parks, it does have solitude and peace, especially in the fall and winter. According to a nearby resident, the park is loveliest in the fall. First there is the leaf color, and then, once the leaves are down, you can see the rocky escarpments that give the gorge its rugged beauty. During the winter, the trail is open to cross-country skiing.

Plans are afoot for more trailhead facilities and defined parking areas. For instance, the park's hiking attractions are to be enhanced by interpretive signing of historic and natural features along the river trail. In addition, several other hiking trails are planned along the rim and at the north end of the park.

To keep up with what is happening at this park-on-the-move, you can write to the Lehigh Gorge State Park, R.D. 2, Box 56, Weatherly, PA 18255, or call 717-427-8161. In any case, be sure to stop in the office at Rockport and pick up a mini-map of the park before setting out.

From Interstate 80: Take Exit 40 (White Haven) and follow Pa. 940 west. After 0.6 mile, turn left toward Weatherly. Drive 6.1 miles and then take a sharp left onto Rockport Road. After 1 mile, pull left into the parking lot just beyond the park office.

11   BRISTOL MARSH

To the uninitiated, the 11-acre Bristol Marsh, at the edge of Bristol in Bucks County, looks like any other marshy area along the Delaware River. And so it was, once upon a time, before such places were overwhelmed by industrial and residential development. But today it is one of the last remnants in Pennsylvania of the river's freshwater intertidal marshes, which once stretched from Marcus Hook to Morrisville. Bristol Marsh itself is a truncated piece that previously extended as far as half a mile up nearby Otter Creek.

On a hot August day, great cormorants skim over the Delaware River, while boats of every size and description course back and forth through the water like a restless pod of whales. Gulls call overhead, and on the mudflat you might spot a snowy egret feeding with several Canada geese. Belted kingfishers rattle past, and over the marsh itself zoom white-tailed dragonflies and green darners.

But the plant life of the marsh is the most interesting—especially the six rare-to-Pennsylvania plants, including the also globally rare *Bidens bidentoides*, called the tidal shore beggar's-tick by Robert Mohlenbrock in his *Where Have All the Wildflowers Gone?* This member of the Aster family is restricted to the freshwater tidal marshes and mudflats of the mid-

View of Bristol Marsh.

Atlantic states—hence the first part of its name. The other rare plants include two grasses—salt-marsh cockspur or Walter's barnyard grass (*Echinochloa walteri*), found at only five locations in Bucks and Philadelphia counties, and Indian or northern wild rice (*Zizania aquatica*). In addition, the marsh has two arrowheads: *Sagittaria subulata*, a mat-forming member of the water plantain family, and a variety, *Sagittaria calycina* var. *spongiosa*, the only sample left in Pennsylvania, as well as *Amaranthus cannabinus*, a member of the amaranth family.

During August, three rare plants steal the show. Mats of *Sagittaria subulata*, with its lovely white, three-petaled flowers, hug the ground and are hidden by the exuberance of taller plants, such as the Indian wild rice and the towering amaranth. Because the rice's gourmet grains are eaten by both humans and waterfowl, it is an especially valuable grass. Botanically it is interesting because the male flowers rise on a plumelike inflorescence at the top of its stem, while the female flowers fan out beneath, a characteristic you can easily observe. A more common grass, called spike rush (*Eleocharis acicularis*), grows abundantly in low, foot-high mats. Its scientific name refers to its preferred "marsh" habitat and its "needle-shaped" appearance.

Other common tidal marsh species are also in bloom in August. Smartweeds are represented by *Polygonum hydropiperoides,* or mild water-pepper, which has tiny pink-and-white flowers clustered in a terminal spike, and by its close but prickly relative *Polygonum arifolium* or halberd-leaved tearthumb, sporting small pink-and-white flower clusters with broad, arrow-shaped leaves. The sharp, downward-pointing barbs along its stem are responsible for its name, "tearthumb."

Sweet flag (*Acorus calamus*), a member of the arum family, has rigid swordlike leaves that are fragrant when crushed, hence the "sweet" in sweet flag. On the other hand, the Lenni Lenape Native Americans called it "wisuhkum," meaning "it tastes bitter," and used the juice from its mashed root for heart disease. The plant also has a distinctive club-shaped stalk or spadix that juts out at an angle from the stem and is crowded with tiny yellowish blossoms.

Two members of the Pickerelweed family are also at their height in August: the pickerelweed itself (*Pontederia cordata*), its upright spire of blue flowers emerging from the base of its distinctive arrow-shaped leaves, and mud-plantain (*Heteranthera reniformis*), noted for its wide dark-green, floating leaves and spike of small white or pale-blue flowers. Mud-plantain continues to blossom as late as November because the tides protect the blossoms from early frosts.

While all the previously mentioned wildflowers grow with their feet in the water, so to speak, the bank of the marsh is lined with blue false indigo (*Baptisia australis*), a showy member of the Pea family with distinctive, clover-shaped leaves. Each of its large dark-blue or violet flowers with its own small stalk is arranged singly along an erect raceme.

Without the help of expert botanists, it is difficult to recognize most of the plants, particularly the rare ones, so it is important for visitors to go on guided tours of Bristol Marsh led by knowledgeable naturalists. For a small fee, The Nature Conservancy, which owns the property, leads several tours a year for both members and nonmembers.

The Conservancy also holds periodic cleanups of the marsh, since the tides deposit river trash. During one January trash-removal day, volunteers filled a dumpster. Volunteers have also been busy removing invasive species, which crowd out the rarer plants. In addition, the Conservancy has raised money to build a boardwalk along the edge of the marsh. This will make it easier to show visitors the diversity of the area while keeping feet dry and protecting the plants.

Bristol Marsh can be profitably visited several times a year, although August is a peak time to see the rare plants. For a look at migratory waterfowl, such as black ducks and blue-winged teal, spring and fall are best. Winter is definitely not the time to visit, because the plants are dead and it looks like an unproductive mudflat.

For more information about guided nature walks, call the Philadelphia Field Office of The Nature Conservancy at 215-963-1400.

From the Pennsylvania Turnpike: Follow the turnpike east to Exit 29, the last exit before New Jersey. Take U.S. 13 south and turn left on Bath Road at the second traffic light (sign for hospital and Silver Lake Nature Center). After 2.3 miles, angle left onto Mill Street at stop sign. One block beyond the next traffic light, turn right into a large municipal parking area. Access to the marsh is at the right-hand end of the parking area toward the river. From center-city Philadelphia, follow Interstate 95 north about 18 miles to Pa. 413 for Bristol; south on 413 1.1 miles to U.S. 13; north on Route 13 0.6 mile to Bath Road; turn right on Bath Road.

12   DELHAAS WOODS

"A tiny island of another age," Ann Rhoads, Director of Botany at the Morris Arboretum, calls Delhaas Woods in lower Bucks County. This 181-acre woods, wet meadow, and bog is the largest and best remaining example of Pennsylvania's coastal-plain forest. Now owned and managed by the nearby Silver Lake Nature Center in Bristol, Delhaas Woods, with its 13 rare-to-Pennsylvania plant species, is a veritable treasure trove for botanists.

Pennsylvania's share of the Atlantic Coastal Plain is a narrow strip of land below the fall line dividing the coastal plain from the piedmont and encompassing communities along the Delaware River in southern Bucks County and in Philadelphia and Delaware counties. Even before William Penn arrived in Pennsylvania in 1682, early Swedish and English settlers had already cut most of the coastal-plain forest, using its wood to build their homes and then farming the cleared land. This pattern of heavy use

The edge of Delhaas Woods.

has continued to the present time, and what was not leveled to build Philadelphia has been gradually eliminated by sprawling development both northeast and southwest of the city along the river.

Delhaas Woods survived such rampant development because so much of it is a wetland—a marsh, wet meadow, wet forest, and the only remaining coastal-plain bog in Pennsylvania. This wide range of different habitats in such a small area has led to incredible plant diversity and is the reason the property has so many rare species. But despite its wetness, a former owner, the Bristol Investment Company, had the property for sale on the open market for several years. In the meantime, it was used as a dumping ground by some local people.

Finally, in 1988, The Nature Conservancy's Pennsylvania chapter purchased Delhaas Woods, and then transferred the tract to the Bucks County Parks Department as an addition to the Silver Lake County Park. In 1993 another purchase expanded the property and connected the existing parcels. After the initial purchase, the real work began. First, accessways were blocked to prevent dumping. Next, volunteers initiated the first of several cleanups, assisted by the Maintenance Division of the Bucks County Department of Parks and Recreation. Six 30-yard containers were filled in five hours, and during a second cleanup five more containers were filled. Altogether, a mind-boggling 50 tons of trash were removed from the site.

But now Delhaas Woods looks like a woods instead of a dump, and August is the time to visit if you want to see some of the rare plants in bloom. One of the best areas to check is the wet meadow, a wide swath where trees are kept cut because it is beneath a powerline right-of-way. This allows meadow plants to thrive. There you should find the endangered (in Pennsylvania) Maryland meadow-beauty, *Rhexia mariana*, along with its close relative the Virginia meadow-beauty, *Rhexia virginica*. Both species have several pink, four-petaled flowers with conspicuous yellow stamens atop a one-to-two-foot stem, but the Virginia meadow-beauty flowers are deep rose while the Maryland meadow-beauty is pale pink. To see both growing in clumps side by side is a rare treat, one you can experience in Pennsylvania only at Delhaas Woods.

This wet meadow, interspersed with boggy areas of sphagnum moss, has several other less rare but still beautiful wildflowers, all of which are found primarily on the coastal plain—a Joe-Pye-weed (*Eupatorium dubium*), the only *pink* St. Johnswort, the marsh St. Johnswort (*Hypericum virginicum*), and orange milkwort (*Polygala lutea*).

Orange milkwort is described by Delaware County botanist Jane Scott, in her wonderful book *Botany in the Field,* as looking like "bright clumps of orange lollipops in the sphagnum mat of Coastal Plain bogs." According to Scott, the clover-like blossoms of orange milkwort are extremely long-lasting, continuing to bloom from the center as the dead petals drop from the outer rim. Other wetland species that brighten the meadow are the five-petal rose-pinks, a member of the Gentian family, and the shrubby water willow or swamp loosestrife, sporting tufts of lavender flowers where its leaves join the stem.

In the wet coastal-plain forest itself, look for the distinctive shrubs and trees that like its sandy soils. Along its moist edges grow the sweet pepperbush or summer-sweet, with its dense, slender spikes of fragrant white flowers. Some of the other species that make up the understory include sweet-bay magnolia (also called the swamp or laurel magnolia), fetterbush or swamp leucothoe, American holly, and thickets of greenbrier.

The dominant tree species are sweet gum, umbrella magnolia, red maple, and willow oak. The willow oak (*Quercus phellos*) is primarily a southern species that likes to grow in poorly drained sand or clay soils and has distinctive two-to-four-inch-long, lance-shaped leaves. Delhaas Woods boasts the largest willow oak in Pennsylvania, with a trunk 45 feet in circumference. In fact, that tree is estimated to be 300 years old and is believed to be Pennsylvania's oldest and largest tree.

The sweet-bay magnolia, along with the willow oak, the American holly, and the umbrella magnolia, are all species of special concern in Pennsylvania, because with the exception of the umbrella magnolia they are found only in southeastern Pennsylvania. Another special plant is the netted chain fern, *Woodwardia areolata*, which likes wet woods and swamps, particularly in coastal areas.

There are many more plants to look for in other seasons and other localities, including those remaining species of special concern found so far in Delhaas Woods: the New York aster, spike grass, bull sedge, forked rush, slender sea-oats, Atlantic blue-eyed grass, coast violet, and spotted pondweed.

Although the Delhaas Woods is open to casual walking and nature study by any interested person, it is best to visit it with experts in order to fully appreciate what you are seeing. Call the Silver Lake Nature Center at 215-923-7400 and find out when they are leading walks into the area. Or stop there first to pick up a map, so you can follow the new trail from the nature center parking lot directly to Delhaas Woods.

When you go, take time to explore some of the trails of the Silver Lake County Park itself. This park too is part of the coastal plain and has two miles of trails crossing a variety of habitats, boasts over 160 species of birds, and has an excellent population of rare red-bellied turtles. In addition, there is a new Nature Center, which has a knowledgeable staff, an exhibit area, a gift and book shop, classroom space, and a reference library and is open Tuesday to Saturday from 10:00 A.M. until 5:00 P.M. and on Sunday from noon to 5:00. For a small fee, the staff provides group programs for all ages. The grounds are open every day from dawn until dusk.

From the Pennsylvania Turnpike: Follow the turnpike east to Exit 29 (the last exit before New Jersey). Take U.S. 13 south and turn right on Bath Road at the second traffic light (sign for hospital and Silver Lake Nature Center). Go 0.75 mile and turn into the Nature Center parking lot next to the third building on the right. From center-city Philadelphia, follow Interstate 95 north about 18 miles to Pa. 413 for Bristol. Drive south on 413 1.1 miles to U.S. 13; north on Route 13 0.6 mile to Bath Road; left on Bath Road (exit to the right on a jug-handle interchange) to the Nature Center.

13   QUAKERTOWN SWAMP

Although Quakertown Swamp, a 400-acre wetland in Upper Bucks County, is primarily in private hands, the former Bucks County Conservancy (now Heritage Conservancy) began studying the area in 1988 as part of their Significant Natural Areas Preservation Program (SNAPP). Their goals were to find out more about the natural values of the wetland and to share their findings with local landowners.

Previously, this broadleaf deciduous-shrub swamp had been listed by the Pennsylvania Natural Diversity Inventory as an imperiled habitat in the commonwealth. In addition, the Pennsylvania Breeding Bird Census found that three species of special concern in the state—the marsh wren, the Virginia rail, and the American bittern—nest there. At least one rare plant species, goldenseal, has also been discovered in the swamp, but as in-depth studies continue, other rare species might surface.

Fortunately, a small portion of the Quakertown Swamp is part of State Game Lands 139 and easily accessible to the public. So is the central portion of the swamp, which is bisected by a little-used railroad line, so you can obtain a good view of the area without trespassing on private property.

First, stop at SGL 139. The centerpiece of this section, just east of Muskrat Road, is a small man-made pond occupied in April by a nesting Canada goose at its far end. Look also for wood ducks, eastern phoebes, blue-gray gnatcatchers, ruby-crowned kinglets, and migrating palm warblers hawking insects. You may even spot an osprey flying in low overhead. Here also is the place where birders in the know go in early evening to listen to the elusive Virginia rails calling from their hiding places in the dense shrubbery beside the pond. Those shrubs include silky dogwood, swamp rose, and buttonbush, all indicators of a shrub swamp habitat.

Most of the April wildflowers that like moisture grow along the trail into and away from the pond—spring beauty, trout-lilies, bloodroot, hepatica, rue anemone, long-spurred and yellow violets, false Solomon's seal, perfoliate bellwort, cut-leaved toothwort, and jack-in-the-pulpit. Appropriately enough, yellow loosestrife (also known as "swamp candles") is abundant there in June.

Wetland on State Game Lands 139. Quakertown Swamp.

Continue due east through the game lands until you reach the railroad bed (alternatively, walk east on Rich Hill Road 0.3 mile and turn left onto the railroad tracks), then follow the tracks in a northwesterly direction for half a mile. Because the railroad bed is raised above the wetland, it offers a fine overview of a cattail marsh to the right and a shrub swamp on the left. Both sides gleam with the gold of numerous clumps of marsh marigolds, sunlike focal points for a rainy April day.

Here you should search for the meadowlark-sized, rusty-colored Virginia rail and the larger, green-backed herons. Overhead, look for turkey vultures and possibly an osprey. Canada geese nest here too, sitting triumphantly on nests built atop the numerous muskrat lodges. Altogether the area provides a breeding habitat for at least 10 species of ducks, herons, and marsh birds. Reptiles and amphibians, including six species each of snakes and turtles and five species of salamanders, toads, and frogs, have been recorded in or near Quakertown Swamp. All these common species, such as the midland painted, spotted, and wood turtles, and the spotted, northern dusky, red-backed, and northern two-line salamanders, are an important part of a diverse ecosystem, even if they are not rare.

It is difficult to believe that much in the swamp has changed since settlers first moved into the area. Indeed, despite settlement in the early eighteenth century by English Quakers, the swamp was relatively undisturbed over the years. First local potters used its clay to make pots, particularly the distinctive Pennsylvania German tulipware. Later, hills in the Big Run drainage area, the tributary of the Tohickon Creek, which flows through the swamp, were quarried. The railroad dates from the 1800s, and an old trash dump—a relic of our throwaway society—occupies a portion of the shrub swamp on its southern edge below the tracks. One commercial venture, a muskrat farm, flourished there in the 1930s.

But considering the press of humanity around the area, the continued integrity of this area as a viable swamp could be threatened. Fortunately most of the 32 landowners, while not interested in selling to the Game Commission, do not want to sell to commercial interests either. For instance, the Paletown Rod and Gun Club, which owns 17.5 acres of the wetland, has been propagating ducks on its property. Members of the club have attended meetings and outings held by the Heritage Conservancy to educate the public about the swamp's natural values.

Finish your outing on another portion of the State Game Lands just north of Rocky Ridge Road. After following a wide strip of mowed grass, you will dead-end at a small scenic swamp with a wilderness look and feel, despite the abundance of duck nesting boxes. In April you will probably find only mallard pairs in the area, but later in the year both mallards and wood ducks nest there. By then the shrubs and trees have leafed out, the waters of the swamp are occupied by snapping turtles and northern water snakes, and the air above hums with mosquitoes.

At the height of its productivity, this swamp serves as a nursery for what many people consider the "good" creatures (ducks) and the "bad" creatures (snakes, snapping turtles, mosquitoes). Instead of being cherished for their diversity and productivity, such places are still loathed by most of our "use-oriented" society. But without such wild places in a rapidly urbanizing area, future generations will live greatly diminished lives.

From Exit 32 of the Northeast Extension of the Pennsylvania Turnpike: Follow Pa. 663 north 3.2 miles toward Quakertown to the intersection with Pa. 309. Turn right (south) on 309. After 2.7 miles, turn left onto Rich Hill Road. Cross Old Bethlehem Road at the stop sign and proceed straight ahead. After 1.3 miles from Route 309, turn left onto Muskrat Road, and after another 100 feet turn right into the State Game Land 139 parking area. To reach the portion of state game lands north of Rocky Ridge Road from the parking lot, go back to Rich Hill Road, turn left, and follow it east and then north 1 mile to the intersection of Rocky Ridge Road. Turn left and go 0.3 mile, then turn right into a game commission pull-off.

14   WILDWOOD LAKE

How often we have flashed past the lower end of Wildwood Lake on Interstate 81 in North Harrisburg and never noticed it. Managed by the Dauphin County Parks and Recreation Department, the 76-acre Wildwood Lake is hemmed in by superhighways, railroad tracks, and factory warehouses. Yet the lake and its surrounding wooded parkland are a haven for wildlife and native plants.

Wildwood Lake was once called Wetzel's Swamp, but in 1908 the major stream within the swamp, Paxton Creek, was dammed to create a recreational lake. At that time the new lake had an average depth of 4 feet

American lotus (right) and swamp rose-mallow (left). Wildwood Lake.

with a maximum of 13 feet, sufficient for the leisurely boating and canoeing people enjoyed in the days before powerboats. Over the years, however, the lake filled with sediment and is now no deeper than a foot and a half in most areas, having reverted back to its swampy origins.

In early spring, when water levels are highest and vegetation is still in bud, the illusion of a lake remains. The water gyrates with spawning carp. Painted turtles sun on logs jutting out into the lake. The weedy margins buzz with red-winged blackbirds, and great egrets stand in silhouette, their striking white plumage lighting up an overcast April morning. So it was the first time we visited Wildwood Lake.

Park at the small lot labeled "Wildwood Lake Nature Center," which has a modest couple of picnic tables, and take the circular, 3.1-mile-long path around the lake. At first the continual traffic noise may bother you, but soon you will be busy watching yellow-rumped warblers in the woodland trees and identifying the waterfowl on the lake—mallards, blue-winged teal, wood ducks, Canada geese, and great blue herons, to name only a few of the possibilities in early spring.

To reach the eastern side, once you reach the end of the western side, follow a blocked-off road around the upper edge until it crosses East Shore Trail. Along that trail a wide assortment of spring wildflowers bloom—beds of trout-lilies and mayapples, an entire hillside of cut-leaved toothworts and Dutchman's breeches, clumps of yellow violets and spring beauties.

But to see the outstanding attraction at Wildwood Lake, you must visit in August, when the lake is almost covered by two species of wild water-lilies. The common fragrant water-lily (*Nymphaea odorata*) has showy white flowers three to five inches in width, and floating heart-shaped leaves. The Pennsylvania-endangered American lotus (*Nelumbo lutea*) has four-to-eight-inch-wide, pale-yellow blossoms and large bowl-shaped leaves. Another showy wildflower, growing along the marshy edges of the lake, is the swamp rose-mallow (*Hibiscus moscheutos*), with spectacular five-petaled, carmine-centered white flowers.

Except for a much smaller number of American lotus at Pymatuning Lake in northwestern Pennsylvania, the American lotus at Wildwood Lake is the only known wild population of the flower in Pennsylvania. Also called "water chinquapin," it is found along the Gulf Coast and in the central and eastern United States as far north as Minnesota, Michigan, and Massachusetts, but it remains an uncommon species except in the Mississippi Valley, where it is abundant in oxbow lakes, sloughs, and ponds. American lotus grows in still water with a mud bottom, certainly the kind of habitat Wildwood Lake now has to offer.

Ecologist Bill Ettinger, after exhaustive interviews with local residents, is still not certain when American lotus first appeared on the lake and whether it came on its own or was planted. Like the sacred lotus (*Nelumbo nucifera*) of Asia and Australia, introduced into the United States by the nursery trade, the American lotus is a popular ornamental in water gardens and easily available through commercial sources.

Ettinger did find definite proof, through the diary of local amateur botanist Paul Walker, that the American lotus covered at least an acre on the east side of the lake by 1958. "Wildwood Lake," Walker wrote in disgust nine years later, "is a mass of American lotus, cattails, pond lilies, gradually turning into a swamp." Other local residents Ettinger talked to declared they had seen American lotus at the lake as early as the 1920s.

Whatever its origin, the American lotus has changed the character and altered the wildlife of the lake. Its seeds, which are viable for many years, are relished by waterfowl. Muskrats also eat it and use its stems for their winter lodges. When there is abundant American lotus in the lake—Ettinger has established through study and aerial photography that the lotus beds have waxed and waned over the last several decades—the lotus colonies provide important nurseries for fish and other aquatic life, as well as shelter for ducks.

Wildwood Lake, supporting abundant wildlife and an endangered Pennsylvania plant, is the kind of wetland that, because of its accessibility, should arouse the interest of a wide variety of outdoor-oriented people in the importance of protecting wetlands from further human encroachment.

From Harrisburg: Follow Front Street north 4 miles to Pa. 39. Turn right on 39 east. Drive 0.2 mile, and just before crossing a bridge over U.S. 22/322, turn right into an industrial-park access road. The entrance to Wildwood Lake Nature Center is on the left after 100 yards.

15 TUCQUAN GLEN / PYFER NATURE PRESERVES

Tucquan means "winding water," an apt name for a creek that winds seven miles from gentle upland headwaters to rocky cascades as it approaches the Susquehanna River. All of it, including the Clark's Run tributary, is classified in Pennsylvania as a Scenic River. Tucquan Glen, located between nearby Kelly's Run Natural Area to the south and Shenk's Ferry Glen Wildflower Preserve to the north, is one of several picturesque glens in Lancaster County. It too has a variety of early-spring wildflower, fern, and tree species.

In a series of purchases during the 1980s, the Lancaster County Conservancy preserved 111 acres below River Road and 31 acres above. Although you can explore the upper, trail-less portion, the lower section of the glen is more easily accessible on a 1.5-mile trail that leads down through the glen to the river. As you face the area from River Road, you should stay on the right-hand side of the stream and follow a trail that sometimes meanders steeply up and over hillsides and at other times utilizes the flat portions of an old jeep trail. In the spring the trail is slippery and wet in places, so good footgear is necessary.

The creek itself follows the fault lines in the underlying Wissahickon schist and finally cascades over large fallen blocks of this rock. Steep wooded slopes to the right of the trail provide a cool, moist growing

Tucquan Creek. Tucquan Glen/Pyfer Nature Preserves.

medium for 21 fern species, including three that are considered rare. More than 40 early-spring wildflower species grow in the glen itself, overshadowed by at least 40 tree species.

During our late-April visit we found a good selection of wildflowers—rue anemones, spring beauties, purple and large-flowered trilliums, wild geraniums, Canada mayflowers, early saxifrages, false and true Solomon's seals, smooth yellow violets, jack-in-the-pulpits, Indian cucumber-roots, wild ginger, trout-lilies, dwarf ginseng, yellow mandarins, hepaticas, and large-flowered bellworts. But we missed many others, including bloodroot, false hellebore, and cut-leaved toothwort.

The gorge is wildly beautiful, and in places rings with the singing of Louisiana waterthrushes. Other birds we heard were wood thrushes, red-bellied woodpeckers, Canada geese flying overhead, one belted kingfisher near the river, and the usual cacophony of blue jays. But mostly the sound of running water drowns out birdsong.

Walking along, you eventually enter what appears to be the mouth of the gorge, where the creek loops left and there is no way to continue along the stream (unless you want to wade in it). Instead, take the trail on the right bank to the top of the hill for a view of the gorge below, half-hidden by a dense cover of hemlock and rhododendron. Then continue ahead down the trail for a pristine view of the Susquehanna River in front of and below you. On this portion of the trail, lady, Christmas, and ostrich ferns cascade down the banks along with an eye-catching display of blue phlox (*Phlox divaricata*).

Although you can walk to the river's edge, halfway down the final descent we turned around and retraced our steps through the gorge. On the return trip, we paid more attention to the diversity of tree and shrub species, admiring the fine stands of tulip poplar, American beech, several hickory species, red and chestnut oak, and black and yellow birch.

Of particular interest is the common papaw, an upright shrub or small tree, usually 5 to 15 feet high. Its large, drooping, ovate leaves with pointed tips are similar to the leaves of many tropical trees, probably because common papaw (*Asimina triloba*) is a member of the tropical Custard Apple family, the only member to range so far north. In March or April it bears three-part greenish blossoms, which turn brown and then a dark wine color with the odor of fermenting grapes. These flowers grow along the previous season's branchlets. From the flowers, thick oblong berries two and a half to five inches long with yellowish-green to dark-brown skin develop and ripen in October. Because they look like stubby bananas, the shrub is also called the wild banana tree. When the fruit is nearly black,

wrinkled, and rotten-looking, the yellow or orange flesh is finally soft, cus-
tardy, and palatable. A favorite of southern Native Americans, who often
cultivated them, papaws were made into a jelly by early settlers. Although
the seeds contain a powerful alkaloid that has a stupefying effect on animal
brains, opossums, raccoons, and gray squirrels relish the fruit.

Other shrubs to look for are common spicebush and several species of
viburnums. We also found the dark-green and white-checkered leaves of
downy rattlesnake plantains still sporting their dried seed-heads from the
summer before. Best of all, though, is the hillside blanketed with large-
flowered trilliums, *the* spring signature species of this spectacular glen.

*From Lancaster: Follow U.S. 222 south for 3.8 miles. Continue straight ahead on
Pa. 272 for 8.5 miles and turn right on Pa. 372 toward Holtwood. After 4.8 miles,
turn right on River Road. Follow River Road north for 2.7 miles to the gorge
entrance on the left.*

16   KELLY'S RUN NATURAL AREA AND SHENK'S FERRY GLEN WILDFLOWER PRESERVE

Because of the 295-foot drop in elevation from the Susquehanna River
Falls at Harrisburg to the headwaters of the Chesapeake Bay, several wa-
terpower dams have been built to create "steps" on the river's fall. Gazing
down at the river from the Face Rock Observation Site on the eastern
shore of the Susquehanna, you can see water managed mostly for human
use—in other words, a tamed river. But Pennsylvania Power & Light,
builder of the Holtwood Dam, has managed to save natural glens on both
sides of the river: Otter Creek to the west and Kelly's Run and Shenk's
Ferry Glen Wildflower Preserve to the east in southern Lancaster County.

Kelly's Run and Shenk's Ferry Glen Wildflower Preserve are as spectac-

View along Kelly's Run. Kelly's Run Natural Area.

ular and varied as Otter Creek, which was covered in *Outbound Journeys in Pennsylvania*. Tucked into the so-called "river hills" of Lancaster County, the two areas are 10 miles apart by road. Combining a visit to both places on a late April or early May day is a good idea if you are interested in seeing many of Pennsylvania's showiest spring wildflowers, along with a rushing mountain stream in a virgin-forest setting.

After picking up brochures at the PP&L Land Management Office entryway, return the half-mile back to the Holtwood Picnic and Recreation Area, where you can park your car and take the two-mile-long, blue-blazed Kelly's Run Trail. At first it winds through a second-growth oak forest of predominately chestnut oak, with some northern red, black, and white oak mixed in, and a heavy understory growth of mountain laurel. In several places you can still see the level, blackened areas now covered with leaf duff, where in the nineteenth century wood was burned in round earth-covered pits to make charcoal.

Once the trail reaches Kelly's Run, after three-quarters of a mile, the character of the land and the vegetation changes. This is mostly a virgin forest of hemlock and tulip trees with an understory of large rhododendron bushes. The rushing mountain stream cuts through a rocky gorge composed of metamorphic Wissahickon schist formed 500 million years ago.

In early spring the water is high and the narrow banks along the stream are strewn with wildflowers. A male Louisiana waterthrush, seeking a mate with which to build a nest along the stream bank, sings loudly enough to be heard over the roar of water. Because the gorge is narrow and the stream frequently overruns its banks, PP&L has found it difficult to maintain the footpath that threads its way in, around, and over enormous boulders. Not wanting to destroy the wild aspect, they used an electric jackhammer, which they brought up the trail in a wheelbarrow, to drill a trail in the rock. This was done so cleverly that the trail seems to be part of the natural rock depressions. Years ago the Civilian Conservation Corps also did some "stream improvement" at one of the water crossings, and that area of flattened pebbles is more noticeable.

Nevertheless, as the stream continues its plunge toward the Susquehanna, the gorge becomes more spectacular. To the right of the stream, you will also find the remains of an old cistern, which was used to water the horses that pulled wagons up this portion of the trail. From there until you reach the road, the banks on both sides of the trail are covered with spring wildflowers, such as early saxifrage, spring beauty, mayapples, jack-in-the-pulpit, Solomon's seal, yellow corydalis, cut-leaved toothwort, wild ginger, and dwarf ginseng.

For an even more overwhelming display of wildflowers, retrace your steps to where you parked your car and drive 10 miles north to the Shenk's Ferry Glen Wildflower Preserve. There the softer, nutrient-rich Conestoga limestone has protruded over the harder schist and created, along Grubb Run, hillsides covered with more than 73 species of woodland wildflowers. The main hiking trail through the 30-acre glen, once the bed of a narrow-gauge railroad used to haul out iron ore, is level and easy to walk along.

The highlight for visitors in April is probably the thousands and thousands of *Trillium erectum*, red trillium, that blanket the hillsides. However, the flowers are not red but a dull white, one color variation of red trillium that is usually scarce or absent among most stands of *Trillium erectum*. Actually, there is some controversy among botanists, both amateur and professional, about what species they are. Some claim they are the more midwestern species, *Trillium flexipes* (drooping trillium), and not *Trillium erectum* at all, but botanists at the Morris Arboretum insist they are the latter. Intermixed with the trillium are the mostly pastel blue but occasionally pink blossoms of Virginia bluebells.

Noting the difference between squirrel corn and Dutchman's breeches is another interesting exercise for amateur naturalists, since both are abundant and grow very much together at Shenk's. They are members of the Poppy family and belong to the genus *Dicentra*. Their leaves are similarly feathery and grow in threes. Each has a separate flower stalk supporting five to seven small white flowers tipped in yellow. But the blossoms of Dutchman's breeches (*Dicentra cucullaria*) look like the legs of pants hanging upside down, whereas the squirrel corn (*Dicentra canadensis*) flowers are heart-shaped.

Trout-lilies also come in two species at Shenk's. The earlier-blooming yellow trout-lily or adder's-tongue, with its reflexed yellow petals and mottled leaves, is familiar to most people who haunt woodland streams in early spring because they are usually abundant in moist areas close by. Members of the Lily family (*Erythronium americanum*), they flower from March until May. A little later, April until June, a mostly midwestern species, the white trout-lily (*Erythronium albidum*), with its single white, drooping flower and unmottled leaves, also blooms at Shenk's.

Although most people visit Shenk's to see wildflowers, those in the know look for ferns as well. Maidenhair is abundant along the trails, but you have to search a little harder to find the two ledge-loving ferns—the fragile or brittle fern, which has the usual feathery, fernlike appearance, and the very unfernlike evergreen, elongated, leathery leaves of the walking fern. If you look carefully, you might find places where the long, thin points of the triangular leaves, from where new plants sprout, have fastened themselves to the ground—hence the name "walking fern."

Because Shenk's Ferry Glen Wildflower Preserve has such a wide variety of interesting plants, you might need some help identifying them. You can call 717-284-2278 or write to the Holtwood Land Management Office, PP&L, RD 3, Box 345, Holtwood, PA 17532, and ask when the next guided wildflower walk is being held. Pennsylvania Power & Light offers a series of free nature programs at all of its facilities in both York and Lancaster counties, and there is family and group camping at its Otter Creek and Pequea Creek campgrounds.

In addition, tree buffs may want to visit the small Holtwood Arboretum near the Kelly's Run trailhead to see the 43 labeled species there. However, to see the largest and oldest (300 years) American holly tree east of the Mississippi River, you must cross the river and drive a couple of miles south of Otter Creek to the Indian Steps Museum.

A final drawing card to this lovely area is the walk along the remnants of the 45-mile-long canal that operated from 1840 until 1894 between Wrightsville, Pennsylvania, and Havre de Grace, Maryland, now called by PP&L the "Lock 12 Historic Area." Several free guided walks are also offered there. In fact, if you live nearby you should get on the PP&L mailing list for their spring, summer, and fall program brochures. Something is nearly always going on there, and it is usually a natural happening.

From Lancaster: Follow U.S. 222 south for 3.8 miles. Continue straight ahead on Pa. 272 south. After 8.5 miles, turn right on Pa. 372 west toward Holtwood. At 4.8 miles farther, turn right on River Road, then turn left onto Old Holtwood Road after 0.4 mile. Follow Old Holtwood Road another half-mile to the park office on the left. To reach Kelly's Run Trail, drive back up Old Holtwood Road about 200 yards and turn into the picnic area on the left. After hiking the trail, return to your car and head for Shenk's Ferry by driving north on Drytown Road (intersects Old Holtwood Road at the picnic ground) 0.3 mile. Turn left on River Road toward Pinnacle and Pequea. Drive 3.8 miles on River Road. After another 0.1 mile, River Road continues to the left, then doglegs left, then right again, and continues for 1.7 miles to the junction with Pa. 324. Turn left, cross Pequea Creek, and after 0.1 mile turn right on River Road. Proceed 1.9 miles. Turn left on Shenk's Ferry Road and follow it 1.1 miles. Turn left on Green Hill Road. After 0.1 mile it becomes a dirt road. Proceed 0.4 mile farther, going under the railroad tracks. Bear left and drive another 0.3 mile. Park near the entrance at Shenk's Ferry.

17   GOAT HILL SERPENTINE BARRENS

A dozen members of The Nature Conservancy stood atop a steep bluff looking at a plant found nowhere else in the world. There, amid pitch pine and red cedar trees, the small white, five-petaled flowers of mouse-ear or long-hairy barrens chickweed (*Cerastium velutinum* var. *villosissimum*) bloomed in mid-May, the dense hair on its leaves helping to insulate it from drying winds and the heat of direct sunlight.

The site of this endemic plant and many other rare species, both plants and moths, is the Goat Hill Serpentine Barrens in southwestern Chester County, one of the best examples of serpentine barrens in the eastern United States. Some 93 acres of the 1,000-acre area have been purchased by The Nature Conservancy. Another 600 acres are owned and managed by the Pennsylvania Bureau of Forestry as a natural area.

Serpentine areas are rare throughout the world, but where they occur the plants that inhabit them are nearly all either endemic to serpentine barrens or disjunct species—that is, species found hundreds of miles away in similar soil communities. In the United States, serpentine outcrops appear only in California and southern Oregon in the west, and southeastern Pennsylvania and north-central Maryland in the east. Goat Hill Barrens and the nearby Nottingham Barrens, preserved by Chester County as a county park, are the two largest serpentine barrens in the eastern United States.

The mineral serpentine is thought to have originated deep in the earth's mantle more than a billion years ago, and to have been squeezed upward by the formation of mountain chains that later eroded away, leaving in some areas exposed serpentine rock rich in magnesium iron silicate. The soils that formed over the rock outcrops are low in the soil nutrients lime and potash and high in toxic-to-plant metals, such as nickel and chromium. Those conditions create a soil so impoverished that most plants cannot grow there.

At the Goat Hill and Nottingham Serpentine Barrens, three categories of plants thrive: prairie grasses, such as prairie dropseed and little blue-

Pitch pine growing amid greenbrier. Goat Hill Serpentine Barrens.

stem, which grow mainly in the midwestern and western United States; trees and herbs, like the black jack oak and post oak more commonly found on the sandy Atlantic Coastal Plain; and tiny plants with rosettes of leaves close to the ground, such as serpentine chickweed and serpentine aster. But the major plant community is the pitch pine on those sites. Taken together, Goat Hill and Nottingham (for Nottingham, see my *Outbound Journeys in Pennsylvania*, pages 75–77) have the largest biodiversity of the serpentine barren communities in Pennsylvania.

Although scientists admit there is still much to learn about serpentine barren ecology, the difference between the surrounding deciduous forests and old fields and the Goat Hill Barrens is obvious to even the most casual visitor. You can literally step from one plant community to another and find very few plants common to both areas. The species that are common to both grow more slowly and are smaller on the barrens' side, an adaptation to the lower soil nutrients.

Many barrens plants are also fire-adaptive, such as pitch pine, which has thick bark that protects its living, inner cambium layer from fire. In addition, pitch pine has cones held together by a wax that needs fire to melt it so its seeds can be released. As a further precaution, pitch pine trunks are studded with buds that sprout and send out leaves only after a fire.

To get a close look at this unique ecosystem, you can either visit Nottingham County Park and follow its extensive trail system, or take a relatively short walk in the Goat Hill Barrens. Because the Goat Hill trails are unmarked and meander in all directions, you should have a compass, or at least be aware of the direction of the sun and the location of the powerline cutting through the area as you walk along.

From the parking lot, follow the wide trail to the left toward the powerline right-of-way and several mobile homes beyond. Then, at the right-of-way, turn right and walk on the trail that parallels the broad right-of-way. In this area you can see the greenish serpentine rock, and in several open places the ground in May is white with the delicate blossoms of the endemic serpentine chickweed and lyre-leaved rock cress growing together. Prairie warblers, common yellowthroats, field sparrows, indigo buntings, blue-gray gnatcatchers, and rufous-sided towhees called and sang during my visit, but frequenters of the barrens also report such birds as whippoorwills, barred owls, and a bevy of resident warbler species—yellow-throated, pine, worm-eating, black-and-white, chestnut-sided, Kentucky, hooded, cerulean, parula, American redstarts, and yellow-breasted chats.

No less than 15 rare moth species inhabit the barrens, along with the threatened-in-Pennsylvania rough green snake, a slender-bodied, non-poisonous, arboreal species between 22 and 32 inches long that is pale green except for a white-to-yellowish-green belly.

When the powerline right-of-way trail opens up into a wide area, you can either continue to follow the right-of-way trail (for the fainthearted) or take the trail to the right, which shortly passes the posted Nature Conservancy signs and crosses over a wooden bridge spanning a small creek. In this wooded area, pitch pine, red cedar, and greenbrier is abundant—the latter creating such a maze that it is nearly impossible to stray from the trail without being heavily scratched by the persistent briers.

Clumps of the lovely moss-pink (creeping phlox), one of the showiest of barrens plants, grow beside the trail along with arrow-leaved violets. Beside the creek, I discovered just-emerging maidenhair fern, which could have been the common species or the Aleutian maidenhair fern, another disjunct species found also in the far north. Later in the season, serpentine asters, round-leaved fameflower (a disjunct southern species with succulent leaves), plain ragwort, whorled milkweed, and green milkweed, as well as glade spurge, a globally rare and endangered species, and the Pennsylvania-rare pink milkwort, are just a few of the nearly 220 plants characteristic of the barrens ecosystem a botanically inclined visitor can find.

Continue along the unmarked trail, always keeping left, and eventually you will end up back in the open area, having circled through a small portion of both the Bureau of Forestry tract and The Nature Conservancy tract. Retrace your steps back to the parking lot.

The Goat Hill Serpentine Barrens were mined for their magnesite and chromium years ago, and most of the mining scars have healed. But in 1979, neighbors of the barrens learned that a Wilmington-based excavating company was interested in quarrying the serpentine rock. The so-called "Concerned Citizens of West Nottingham Township" opposed not only the quarry but also any further damage to the barrens wilderness surrounding them. Because of their efforts, a large portion of this unique example of our natural heritage, which botanists believe contains the most diverse plant species in all of the 12 Chester County barren sites, now belongs to citizens of the commonwealth and to The Nature Conservancy.

From Lancaster: From the center of the city, follow U.S. 222 south. At 3.8 miles, continue south on Pa. 272 for 20.6 miles, to Wakefield. Turn left and continue 9.5 miles, following 272 into Nottingham. At the stop sign, make a sharp right (sign indicates Nottingham Park). Turn right again 0.4 mile farther and follow the road another 0.9 mile to the park entrance on the left. To reach Goat Hill, go straight ahead on the park road 1.4 miles to a stop sign. Continue straight, then bear left after 0.1 mile, cross a narrow bridge, and follow Lees Bridge Road 1.2 miles to an unmarked paved road to the left. Proceed 100 yards up the hill and turn left again. Drive 0.7 mile more and watch for the Goat Hill Barrens parking lot on the right.

From Philadelphia: Follow U.S. Route 1 south 48 miles to the Nottingham Exit, Route 272. Follow 272 one-half mile east into Nottingham and continue as above.

18   CHROME
SERPENTINE BARRENS

Just north of the Mason-Dixon line in Chester County, The Nature Conservancy has purchased the 225-acre Chrome Serpentine Barrens as part

A spring burn in early autumn. Chrome Serpentine Barrens.

of its goal "to protect a network of potentially connected serpentine barren sites and to restore and maintain them in their natural state." Altogether, the Chrome Serpentine Barrens, along with Nottingham, Goat Hill, and a fourth barren called New Texas, comprise not only the largest expanse of serpentine barrens in the eastern United States, but also the largest area of true prairie and savanna in Pennsylvania.

Such areas were historically maintained by natural fires, because the native plants and trees that inhabit barrens and prairies are highly flammable. This characteristic promotes cool fires, which are harmless to them and their offspring but kill off invading old-field and young-woods competitors. In many cases, barrens species such as pitch pine, scrub oak, and prairie dropseed actually need fire to germinate. So although the Chrome Serpentine Barrens is now owned by Elk Township, The Nature Conservancy, as caretakers of the property, is using it to experiment with prescribed burning management. Their plan is ultimately to restore this habitat to its pre-European settlement condition.

Already they have trained volunteers and staff in proper ecological burning techniques through comprehensive workshops, which include the study of fire weather, fire behavior, smoke management, how to start and put out fires, and the effects burning will have on the plant community. Before their first burn—the first prescribed burn by The Nature Conservancy in Pennsylvania—they cleared fire breaks and removed six truckloads of trash. They also explained their techniques to nearby neighbors and won their support. Then, under the direction of the Conservancy's national fire coordinator, with the assistance of the Pennsylvania Bureau of Forestry and emergency backup from the nearby Oxford Fire Department if needed, they held the first of several planned, controlled fires in an effort to burn off such invasives as juniper, green-brier, and red maples, along with the leaf litter that supports their growth.

Choosing the proper time to burn is a difficult process and depends on the levels of humidity, wind, and ground moisture that are necessary for a thorough and safe burn on what was a relatively small portion of the property—10 acres. At other Nature Conservancy–owned properties, much larger burns are prescribed—for instance, Oklahoma's Tallgrass Prairie Reserve, where 6,000 acres were burned at once. So far, the burns at Chrome seem to be slowly eliminating the competition, but because burning such sites is still experimental, and big gaps still exist in the understanding of fire ecology, especially its precise effects on plants, animals, and barren soils, the approach is slow and easy.

In addition to fire management, the Conservancy also trained volunteers to collect seeds from Goat Hill's abundant prairie grasses—Indian grass, little bluestem, and big bluestem—and to plant them in Chrome's old fields, which they are trying to restore. So far the seeds have germinated well, but biannual grasses require two growing seasons to become fully established.

Restoration management takes many years to accomplish, so visitors to the Chrome Serpentine Barrens can chart the changes from year to year and from burn to burn. After parking in the lot, from the gate go straight ahead to the open area. Then turn right and follow the blue-disk-marked trail. This trail meanders through a good portion of the barrens, past old fields, woods, and areas that have been burned.

During our visit in late August after the first burning had taken place, we found a mixture of invasives, especially green-brier, and serpentine/prairie plants. And as we walked over the flat, almost featureless land, we felt as if we were in the pine barrens of New Jersey, except that the exposed soil and rocks had the telltale greenish-tint of serpentine, which made the system even rarer than the usual remnants of eastern United States barrens areas. In the burn area, though, I spotted familiar coastal-plain trees, black jack oaks (*Quercus marilandica*), along with scrub oaks (*Quercus ilicifolia*). Those two species of fire-dependent, shrubby trees are what define Chrome as the best serpentine site for the scrub oak plant community.

Black jack oak, also known as black oak or barren oak, rarely grows taller than 20 to 30 feet and has a short, thin trunk with stout, short, grotesquely contorted branches. Its distinctive leaves are nearly as broad as they are long and have three shallow lobes near the top. Although it is common in barren, dry, sterile, sandy-to-clay soils throughout the Atlantic Coastal Plain and Piedmont regions, in Pennsylvania it occurs only in the southeastern part of the commonwealth.

Scrub oak is far more common in the state, springing up in extensive areas following forest fires, or occupying barren mountaintops and rocky slopes—inhospitable, dry, and sterile places, where it usually forms a dense protective cover. Also called bear oak, because its abundant acorns are relished by bears as well as wild turkeys, ruffed grouse, and white-tailed deer, scrub oak is even smaller than black jack oak, usually from 3 to 10 feet in height, but again with a short trunk and stiff, contorted branches.

Although the distinctive trees were easy to locate, we were not lucky enough to find the three rare plants growing only at Chrome. The first is Bicknell's hoary rockrose (*Helianthemum bicknellii*). One of several frostweeds, it is so named because late in the season the bark is cracked and strings of ice crystals may emerge from those cracks. It has narrow, pointed leaves on the stem and comparatively large (one inch across) flowers with yellow petals. The second is a deciduous shrub, staggerbush (*Lyonia mariana*), which grows from eight inches to four feet high and has slender, upright branches. Staggerbush is another mostly coastal-plain species, which in May or June bears nodding, bell-shaped white or pale-pink flowers that later produce urn-shaped, ovoid fruit capsules. Its bright-green, smooth leaves are supposed to be poisonous to lambs and calves—hence the name "staggerbush." The discovery of Curtis's milk-wort (*Polygala curtissii*), the third rare plant at Chrome, was the first Pennsylvania record of this attractive coastal-plain species, which ranges from Delaware to Georgia and Louisiana and inland from West Virginia to Ohio and Kentucky. Its rose-purple petals are tipped in yellow, and it blooms from June to October.

We were also too early to see the serpentine asters in bloom, but we did come across whorled milkweed (*Asclepias verticillata*). This milkweed species does have the usual hourglass-shaped flowers of the milkweed genus, but not the usual stiff, leathery leaves of the common milkweed. Instead, it sports linear leaves in whorls of three to seven, and its greenish-white flower clusters grow in the leaf axils. Ranging over the eastern half of the United States, whorled milkweed is especially abundant in all dry prairie areas.

The other wildflowers in bloom were typical common late-summer species—silver-rod, ironweed, Queen Anne's lace, Joe-Pye-weed, and bone-set, for instance, as well as the showy rose-pink, which grew only in wet, boggy areas. Instead of the rare moth species that serpentine barrens are noted for, the ironweed was covered with tiger swallowtail and red-spotted purple butterflies, and a meadow fritillary fed on a boneset.

The birds too were undistinguished. Turkey vultures wheeled over-head, along with a screaming red-tailed hawk. Blue jays, rufous-sided towhees, mourning doves, Carolina wrens, and a red-bellied woodpecker were also vocal.

So, at this point, a visit to the Chrome Serpentine Barrens mixes the familiar with the unfamiliar. It is The Nature Conservancy's hope that someday the unfamiliar will predominate.

From Lancaster: Follow U.S. 222 (Prince Street) south and, 3.8 miles from the city center, take Pa. 272 south. Turn left off the main highway at Wakefield, 20.6 miles from downtown Lancaster, and continue east on Pa. 272. Route 272 crosses U.S. 1 at Nottingham, 9.1 miles from the turn at Wakefield. Continue straight through Nottingham on 272 to a stop sign at Chrome, 2.5 miles from the U.S. 1 intersection. Turn left, proceed north 0.1 mile and turn on Media Road, the first road to the right. After 1 mile, take Media Road at the stop sign to the right. Drive 0.8 mile farther and turn right on Barrens Road. Follow Barrens Road 0.8 mile to the entrance to the parking area on the left.

From the Philadelphia area, follow Route 1 southeast to the 272 intersection, ap-proximately 4 miles beyond Oxford and 18 miles beyond Kennett Square.

CENTRAL PENNSYLVANIA

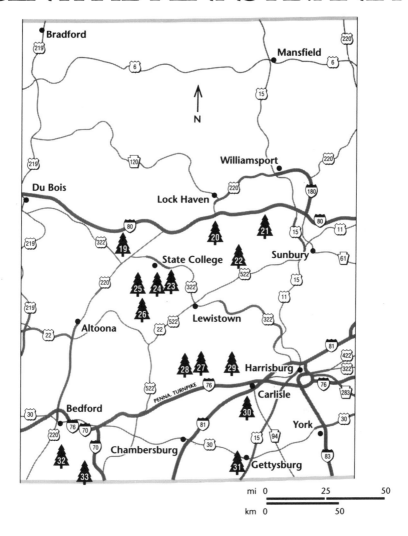

19. BLACK MOSHANNON STATE PARK
20. CHERRY RUN
21. THE HOOK NATURAL AREA
22. SNYDER-MIDDLESWARTH NATURAL AREA
23. DETWEILER RUN NATURAL AREA
24. BIG FLAT LAUREL NATURAL AREA
25. SHAVER'S CREEK ENVIRONMENTAL CENTER
26. ROCKY RIDGE NATURAL AREA
27. FRANK E. MASLAND JR. NATURAL AREA
28. HEMLOCKS NATURAL AREA
29. WAGGONER'S GAP
30. HOLLY GAP PRESERVE
31. GETTYSBURG NATIONAL MILITARY PARK
32. SWEET ROOT NATURAL AREA
33. SIDELING HILL CREEK NATURAL AREA

19   BLACK MOSHANNON STATE PARK

Black Moshannon State Park, in western Centre County, is a park for all seasons. Located on the Allegheny Plateau, the 3,750-acre park has an average elevation of 1,900 feet above sea level. This means that its 250-acre dammed lake is one of the first in the state to freeze over, so winter sports enthusiasts head there to ice-fish, snowmobile, ice-skate, and cross-country ski. With snowfall ranging between 35 and 60 inches most years and beginning to accumulate by the end of December, visitors can depend on a cold, wintery landscape for more than three months of the year.

When we visited the park in early February, there was at least a foot and a half of snow on the ground. The lake was dotted with ice-fishermen, and the two-acre ice-skating area, which is kept plowed, was filled with skaters of all ages. We parked at the end of West Side Road, as close as we could get to the Moss-Hanne Trail and the 1,992-acre Black Moshannon Bog Natural Area.

Despite the relatively large number of people in the lake area that cold, clear winter day, there were only a few cross-country skiers on Indian Trail, which we followed northwest for less than half a mile until we reached the Moss-Hanne Trail to our left. Even though we had forgotten our snowshoes, we were able to walk on the frozen cross-country ski base of both the Indian Trail and the nine-mile Moss-Hanne Trail for several miles, only occasionally sinking up to our knees when we strayed off the trail.

The wind soughed through the evergreens, a large red-pine plantation to our right, and natural regeneration of white pine and spruce on our left. Above the wind we could hear black-capped chickadees and blue jays. The Moss-Hanne Trail had more signs of wildlife than humans— abundant squirrel, deer, grouse, rabbit, and mice tracks, as well as a snow-covered beaver lodge. Eventually the hardened ski trail petered out, but on skis or snowshoes this trail is easily navigable. It is also the most interesting for naturalists because it penetrates the heart of the Black

Beaver lodge in winter. Black Moshannon State Park.

Moshannon Bog Natural Area. One of the first nine state-park designated natural areas, botanists consider this bog area to be "the best reconstituted bog in the high plateau region." Others call it "the heart of Black Moshannon State Park."

"Moshannon" comes from the Indian "Moss-hanne," which means "moose stream," but instead of moose the park supports a healthy number of beaver. Beaver, in fact, built the first dam on Black Moshannon Stream, before the 1850 lumber-camp dam. Once a primeval forest of primarily white pine and hemlock, the area was eventually clear-cut. Only the remnants of three- to five-foot-diameter stumps remain in the reforested second- and third-growth hardwoods, conifer plantations, and scattered portions of mature forest.

In late June, the aspect Black Moshannon State Park presents is different from winter, but equally fascinating. Wildflowers are abundant, and purple fringed orchids are one of the highlights, even growing near the campgrounds. During an early evening walk, a park naturalist showed us a section of the Bog Natural Area that had 57 blooming purple fringed orchids (*Platanthera fimbriata*) and two white varieties of the same species. The woods themselves held many colder-climate wildflowers— bunchberry, goldthread, starflower, and Canada mayflower. The sought-after purple fringed orchids grew in sphagnum moss with Canada mayflowers and cinnamon, interrupted, and sensitive ferns along a tiny stream.

As soon as we left the car to visit the Bog Natural Area, we were serenaded by hermit thrushes. In fact, the hermit thrush remained the premier bird of the park, because no matter where we went (and we made several stops) there were singing hermit thrushes. Ovenbirds and red-eyed vireos were the other, less melodious, deep-woods evening singers.

The park naturalist led us toward the open bog area to give us a good look at an active beaver lodge. Those in the lead even had a quick look at a swimming beaver. In addition, we closely examined the beaver dam itself as cedar waxwings called overhead, bullfrogs croaked, and a ruffed grouse with young exploded out of the underbrush. The naturalist had spent a good deal of time watching this particular lodge over the years, and he showed us how the surrounding area had been changed into a meadow by beaver, which had cut down all the alder trees. He also pointed out places where the sod had been freshly ripped up by beaver to use in their lodge and dam reinforcements. The beaver, and the plentiful black bears, are the most exciting mammal species at Black Moshannon State Park.

Hiking back to our cars, we passed both wood-sorrel and several pink lady's slippers on the way. The bog also supports the insectivorous pitcher plant and round-leaved sundew, both of which bloom in the park in late July. Along the road, we stopped at a wetland covered with scouring rush, *Equisetum hyemale*, a member of the Horsetail family. The wetland rang with the alarm calls of nesting red-winged blackbirds. At the lakeshore itself we found such wildflowers as bluets, dwarf or smaller forget-me-nots, and marsh speedwell. Common yellowthroats, song sparrows, and gray catbirds sang as a light rain fell while the sun still shone. We could see the individual droplets hitting the lake, and turned to find a perfect rainbow in the sky behind us.

Sharper eyes than mine found not one but two wide-leaved ladies'-tresses, *Spiranthes lucida*, growing on the lakeshore. Actually, the botanists in our group, 10-power hand lenses around their necks, debated the identification because none of us could see the fine green lines on the lip of the inconspicuous white flowers, which were supposed to distinguish this species from other ladies'-tresses. On the other hand, the plants had the wide leaves of their name and they are the only inland ladies'-tresses species that bloom in early summer. All the others are late summer and autumn bloomers.

As the sun set over the lake, the naturalist pointed out that there were no mosquitoes. He attributes that to an abundance of still another insectivorous plant—greater bladderwort—some of which he fished out of the lake water to show us. He thinks it lives on mosquito larvae in the spring, which would account for the surprising absence of the pesky insects in the wetland-dominated park.

Similar naturalist-led walks are available to park visitors from Memorial Day to Labor Day. In addition to a family campground and an organized group camping area, you can rent rustic cabins from April through December, and modern cabins year-round. Both hunting and trapping are allowed at the park in season, and fishing, canoeing, picnicking, and swimming are warm-weather options.

Sixteen miles of hiking trails and 6.3 miles of snowmobile trails (in widely separated portions of the park) complete the recreational possibilities at this all-weather facility. Of particular interest is the Bog Trail, a wheelchair-accessible boardwalk that everyone can enjoy. This one-fifth-mile elevated wood walkway makes it easy to observe blooming pitcher plants, leatherleaf shrubs, and cottongrass, as well as two beaver lodges in the distance, without getting your feet wet. Birdwatching is also excellent, especially if you move quietly and slowly. Because the park personnel want to impress on visitors the importance of wetlands, there are also guided walks along the Bog Trail led by knowledgeable naturalists. Altogether, naturally speaking, the wide diversity of plant and animal life is Black Moshannon State Park's greatest drawing card.

For further information about park programs and renting cabins, call 814-342-5960. You can also write Black Moshannon State Park, R.D. 1, Box 183, Philipsburg, PA 16866, for a copy of the cabin rates for the year.

From State College: Follow North Atherton Street, U.S. 322, 9 miles west to the intersection with U.S. 220. Take 220 north 4.8 miles and turn left on the Julian Pike. A sign for the park marks the intersection. The Julian Pike ascends the Allegheny Plateau and intersects Pa. 504 after 8.4 miles. Shortly before that intersection, look for the park office on the right, where you can pick up a map of the park. Turn left on 504, cross the bridge over the lake, and turn left again after 100 yards. Follow this road along the west side of the lake for 1.3 miles, to the parking area at the end of the road, for easy access to the Moss-Hanne Trail.

20   CHERRY RUN

Cherry Run, State Game Lands 295, in Clinton and Centre counties is a 12,670-acre tract of roadless forest paralleling the famed trout stream known as Cherry Run. Because of its pure water and remoteness, the Pennsylvania Fish and Boat Commission has designated it a "Wilderness Trout Stream." As streams go, Cherry Run is not very wide, but it is filled with clear, deep pools beloved by trout and trout fishers. Originally purchased by the Western Pennsylvania Conservancy in 1979, this property was their largest land-conservation venture in their first 50 years. Cherry Run was then turned over to the Game Commission as a wilderness tract.

The 20-square-mile acquisition is flanked by Big Mountain and Bear Mountain and includes four other mountain streams beside Cherry Run. The trail that penetrates the narrow Cherry Run valley itself is an old gated road, so the walking is never difficult. It is somewhat reminiscent

Along Cherry Run. Cherry Run Natural Area.

of Stony Creek near Harrisburg, except that both Cherry Run and its road-trail are narrower and the area less heavily used. Evidences of humanity are few: the remains of a single old shack and a couple of makeshift stone fireplaces near the stream.

Cherry Run is often screened from the trail, and you must make an effort to leave it and go down to the stream bank. Some of the easy-access points are noted with double blazes on the trees, but others you must judge for yourself. Occasionally the way may be blocked by a maze of rhododendron shrubs.

Picturesque as it is, the stream is not the only attraction at Cherry Run. The plants and trees are also of interest. From the parking area, the trail follows Cherry Run upstream a short way and then crosses it and turns left on an old logging road through a planted white pine grove. Soon hemlock becomes the dominant evergreen tree, while tulip, red and sugar maples, black cherry, and yellow birch are some of the most common hardwood species. Because the trail is on the north-facing side of Bear Mountain, it is shady and moist, making it an outstanding place for mosses, including sphagnum, four species of clubmoss (*Lycopodiums*)—running, shining, wolf claw, and tree—and moisture-loving fall flowers, such as closed gentian and turtlehead.

In the spring, Indian cucumber-root, trailing arbutus, Canada may-flower, and several species of violets are common, and the dense shade of summer encourages the growth of the saprophytic Indian pipes as well as sensitive, Christmas, lady, New York, woodland, and cinnamon ferns.

Although the trail roughly follows the south side of Cherry Run, initial views of the stream are soon blocked off by about two miles of dense rhododendron stretching from the trail to the stream bank. Eventually you reach a small, grassy opening that leads down to the stream. There Cherry Run has divided around an island and can be crossed by the sure-footed.

The next break in the rhododendron is advertised by pink blazes on several trailside trees. Beyond that, the character of the woods changes, becoming more open with some white oaks, beeches, and mountain laurel, in addition to all the aforementioned tree and shrub species.

Rocks and fallen logs on the south side of the trail are thickly carpeted by a variegated green rug of mosses and lichens, with three or four species growing beside and on top of one another, including the mountain fern moss, which looks like a blanket of tiny ferns. One researcher in the Adirondacks discovered that mosses grow well on acid soil that is shaded, has a late snow cover, and high humidity—all characteristics of the woods on the south side of the Cherry Run trail.

As you walk along, try to identify birds by their calls, because the dense tree and shrub cover make it almost impossible to spot any species but the fearless black-capped chickadees. Pileated woodpeckers, white and red-breasted nuthatches, golden-crowned kinglets, brown creepers, rufous-sided towhees, blue jays, and common ravens are some of the species you might hear. During the spring and summer, other birders have reported nesting Louisiana waterthrushes along Cherry Run, and hooded warblers in the rhododendron thickets.

Wildlife is almost as difficult to see, although we did surprise white-tailed deer beside the stream. Other possible sightings include black bears, wild turkeys, and eastern coyotes. Along damp sections of the path, especially on an overcast day, look for brilliant orange red eft salamanders, one of the most charming of the salamander tribe.

For an easy hike, walk along the flat trail until your day is half gone, then head back on the same trail, taking plenty of time out for stream-viewing, eating a brown-bag lunch, and dozing in the sun on a grassy bank.

All in all, Cherry Run is the kind of place that can be revisited many times, especially in early July when the rhododendrons which line the trail are in bloom. Their large, showy, pink-and-white blossoms provide a stunning contrast to the almost tropical-green density of the dark forest.

From State College: Proceed approximately 9 miles out of State College northeast on Pa. 26 until you reach Pa. 64. Continue on Route 64 about 9 miles, and just after crossing the intersection with Pa. 445, turn right on the road to Tylersville. After a short distance, at the edge of the village of Lamar, you come to a stop sign. Take a right, still headed toward Tylersville. At 3.4 miles, pull into a Game Commission parking area on the left.

21   THE HOOK
NATURAL AREA

Many Pennsylvania wilderness-lovers believe that The Hook Natural Area in Union County provides the epitome of a wilderness experience. Encompassing 5,119 acres in Bald Eagle State Forest, The Hook Natural Area protects a complete watershed in Pennsylvania's Ridge-and-Valley province and includes two parallel stream valleys, portions of three ridges, and The Hook itself, which is a spectacular water gap. Known only to small numbers of hikers, hunters, and fishers, it is possible to spend a beautiful spring day there and never see another human being. Instead you will see an abundance of birds, wildflowers, ferns, and flowing water.

At first, as you walk down the wide, unnamed path that leads south into the Natural Area, you will see a typical oak-maple forest with a lower story of mountain laurel and low-bush blueberries. In mid-May, rufous-sided towhees, red-eyed vireos, rose-breasted grosbeaks, ovenbirds, and wood pewees, all familiar spring-summer inhabitants of such forests, sing and call against a background of lesser chirps from high-foraging warblers camouflaged by leaves in the topmost treetops.

After about a quarter-mile, a spring emerges from the forest floor on the left and quickly becomes a sizable stream, Panther Run. Just as

Panther Run. The Hook Natural Area.

quickly, the hardwood forest retreats from the stream banks and is replaced by large white pine trees growing amid moisture-loving grasses
and sedges. At a wide plank bridge, we watched a brilliant black-winged
male scarlet tanager and listened to the disembodied song of an un-
known warbler.

From there, the trail continues only a short distance, with Panther Run
still to the left before it reaches a series of large stepping-stones that lead
across the stream to an old wide, cobbled railroad bed. That bed serves
as a rough trail, inimical to all feet but those protected by sturdy hiking
boots.

At this juncture, ridges close in on either side. To the left, a rock slide
blankets most of the mountain for close to half a mile, while large hemlock trees growing in beds of sphagnum moss mingle with the white
pines along the stream bank to the right. Immediately across the stream,
a forest-clad ridge looms. Rhododendron bushes begin to dominate the
understory beside Panther Run, but in several places patches of stiff or
bristly clubmoss (*Lycopodium annotinum*) thrive. In fact, at one point an
enormous patch not only covers the forest floor between the trail and
stream, but also continues across on the other side and extends several
hundred feet up the mountain—by far the largest expanse of clubmoss I
have ever seen in the woods. Those evergreen, bristly leaved plants do
prefer to live in cool, moist woods especially beneath the coniferous trees
they resemble in miniature form, even though they are most closely related to ferns.

Because the trail is paved with rocks, it is important to pay close attention to where you place your feet, to avoid tripping. If you are lucky, you
may spot the delicate white blossoms of starflowers seemingly growing
out of the rocks. Each slender stem supports a whorl of shiny, tapering
leaves from which two threadlike stalks emerge. Those stalks each bear a
single fragile, six-or-seven point star-shaped flower. Starflowers (*Trientalis
borealis*), which grow in cool woods and on high slopes, are common in
the northeastern United States and Canada and range as far south as
Virginia in the mountains.

Pick your way carefully around each flower, and pause to scan the rock
slide to your left in search of eastern phoebe nests. They like to cement
their nests beneath rocky ledges, their natural setting before humans introduced bridges and house eaves, which suit them even better.

Eventually the railroad bed peters out, the trail becomes a footpath
once again, and the open rock-slide, which supports only an occasional
white birch tree, is succeeded by a forested slope. Upland or northern
lady ferns thrive in the moist soil to the left of the trail. They are easy to

identify because the lower pair of leaflets on each frond point downward. One variety, *rubellum*, is further distinguished by its pale wine-color stem. Like starflowers, upland lady ferns are also cold-loving plants.

Growing across the trail from them are two other flower species that often blanket northern forest floors—Canada mayflowers and fringed polygala—although they grow in smaller colonies in cool Pennsylvania woods as well.

Shortly after the trail improves, you begin crossing a series of foot-bridges—five in all—which range from very poor log constructions to excellent, recently rebuilt plank bridges. Pick your way carefully over the rotted logs of the first bridge to the right, then follow the flat, grassy trail to a second log bridge, which is in slightly better repair. The third bridge, made of logs, is the best of the three.

The trail continues to be grassy underfoot. There we found dozens of small fluttering, dark-brown skippers in company with numerous brilliant, red-spotted purple butterflies, all attracted to a patch of beige-colored dead sphagnum moss. A closer look (and sniff) indicated the presence of carrion, a great attraction for red-spotted purples.

Ahead to your left is the fourth bridge, the first made of new planks. At the far end of that bridge, to the right, two large, closely related species of fern—the interrupted and the cinnamon—grow in the moist ground. Both in the genus *Osmunda*, each has distinctive fertile leaves that have brown, spore-bearing leaflets in the spring. These fertile leaves make them easy to identify. Those of the interrupted fern grow in the middle of each leaf, and hence "interrupt" the symmetry of the rest of the leaflets. The cinnamon ferns send up several, separate, cinnamon-colored, clublike fertile leaves in the center of each circular cluster of plants.

Finally, cross the fifth bridge over meandering Panther Run. Shortly afterward, it joins the much larger North Branch of Buffalo Creek which comes in from the right. It is possible to follow the creek east for several miles, but instead retrace your steps back over the five bridges. Then, after rock crossings over two narrow feeder streams coming down off the mountain to the right, take a right fork 200 feet beyond the second stream crossing just before you reach the rock-slide area and rocky trail.

This is the Molasses Gap Trail, which leads up a hollow behind the rock-slide slope at your left with a small stream off in the woods to the right. As you near Jones Mountain Road, the stream disappears, but the trail is quite distinct. Once you reach the road, turn left and walk a half-mile back to your car.

Although the walk is less than 3 miles, the area is so beguiling that it is easy to spend most of a day rambling rather than hiking, stopping frequently to soak in the beauty at every peaceful spot, eating a leisurely trail lunch beneath the hemlocks, and stretching out in the sunshine to relax. Such a slow pace does allow you to see only a small portion of The Hook Natural Area, but you should emerge from the experience refreshed and amazed that such a remote place exists so close to civilization.

From Exit 27 of Interstate 80, 18 miles southwest of Williamsport: Follow Pa. 477 south approximately 8 miles to Livonia (intersection with Pa. 192). Turn left (east) on 192 and proceed 5.7 miles to the dam at R. B. Winter State Park. Continue 0.6 mile to Pine Creek Road. Turn right and drive 1.1 miles uphill. Take a sharp left on Jones Mountain Road and enter The Hook Natural Area. At 0.2 mile from the intersection, pull in right to the unmarked dirt road and park.

22   SNYDER-MIDDLESWARTH NATURAL AREA

The Snyder-Middleswarth Natural Area in Bald Eagle State Forest is a 500-acre tract with virgin white pine, hemlock, and pitch pine. This natural area adjoins the Snyder-Middleswarth State Park, an eight-acre picnic grove along picturesque Swift Run. To reach that grove is an adventure in itself, as you follow a labyrinth of progressively more primitive and remote dirt roads. After you turn into the hemlock-enshrouded picnic area, complete with a covered pavilion, pause to read the stone placard that proclaims the Snyder-Middleswarth Natural Area a Registered Natural Landmark—a site that "possesses exceptional value in illustrating the natural history of the United States." Then set off along the Tall Timbers Trail (Tall Timbers is an alternate name for the area), which follows Swift Run upstream.

You are immediately surrounded by enormous virgin hemlock trees. They grow on a steep mountainside blanketed in ferns and mosses, to your right, or crowded along the narrow bank beside the stream. Many

Tall Timbers Trail through old-growth hemlock. Snyder-Middleswarth
Natural Area.

huge trees have fallen down the mountainside, and they too wear a green mantle of moss and fern. Most also serve as nurse trees for future generations and support dozens of foot-high hemlock seedlings. Hemlocks don't seem to need much earth to anchor their shallow roots. One massive tree and a slippery elm grow out of a rock ledge.

On early autumn days, the woods reverberate with katydids. Leaves and hemlock needles rain down with the slightest breeze. Water striders skate across small pools in Swift Run. Winter wrens, their perky tails at a tilt, scuttle amid the debris of fallen trees and branches, occasionally pausing to bob up and down like animated toys.

These tiniest of our wren species have dark-brown backs, heavily barred bellies, and stub tails. They prefer to hunt for insects in low tangles and uprooted trees along stream beds, on their way to the southern United States from their summer nesting grounds in mixed or coniferous forests of the north. But Snyder-Middleswarth is one of the few places in the state with breeding winter wrens, which like dense hemlock stands on steep slopes. Winter wrens are aptly named because sometimes they will spend the winter in Pennsylvania, preferring just the kind of tangled environment the Snyder-Middleswarth Natural Area offers. One early naturalist called them "spirits of the brooks." Continual troops of black-capped chickadees, a downy woodpecker, one screaming blue jay, and a pair of common ravens that soared overhead were the other prominent birds in the area.

The other wild creature we found was a shiny black salamander with a smattering of faint white spots—a slimy salamander that lives in moist wooded ravines or hillsides. It disappeared so quickly under a rock that I did not have a chance to pick it up and see if it lived up to its name "slimy," which refers to skinlike secretions that stick to your hands like glue.

For more than a mile, the trail follows the stream, but you must frequently detour around the massive trees that have smashed across the trail. Those trees are purposely left in place to add to the fertility of the soil. Then you reach a metal sign pointing left across the stream and up the mountainside toward a fire tower. Ignore that, and continue straight ahead on the same trail.

The vegetation slowly changes. Several hobblebushes with their heart-shaped leaves grow along the stream, and some white pines loom among the hemlocks. More hardwoods, such as yellow birch and several oak species, are mixed in with the conifers, while rhododendron and mountain laurel shrubs replace the thick fern and moss beds.

Eventually the trail closes in with laurel, even though blue blazes continue on the trees. It is best to retrace your steps back to the wooden bridge, cross the stream, and turn left, following the trail, which meanders about 75 feet above the stream and eventually back to the parking lot.

The most beautiful feature of the natural area is the sense of the primeval forest, so dense that only thin shafts of sunlight penetrate the slim openings in the dense canopy. It is, after all, the cathedral-like light that is the most compelling vision a virgin forest conveys. This sacred aura is reason enough for seeking out such places.

From State College: Follow U.S. 322 east for 20.5 miles. Then turn left at a sign that says Reeds Gap State Park and drive through the village of Milroy. Continuing to follow the signs toward Reeds Gap State Park, in the center of the village (0.5 mile from 322), turn left again. Drive 0.3 mile farther and bear left, then 0.3 mile more and turn right. After 2.1 miles, turn left and 1.2 miles more, follow the main road, taking a sharp left. After 0.3 mile, turn right onto New Lancaster Valley Road, still on your way to Reeds Gap State Park, and after 2.8 miles continue straight through the park on New Lancaster Valley Road. Drive 7.8 miles beyond the park headquarters until the paved road takes a very sharp right uphill. Do not follow it. Instead, go straight ahead on a dirt road (Locust Ridge Road). A hard-to-see sign does point to Snyder-Middleswarth State Park. After 2.4 miles, turn right onto Swift Run Road toward Troxelville. Continue another 1.9 miles, watching for a very sharp left turn into a gravel road that leads to the picnic area for the park. If you pass a sign for the park on Swift Run Road, you have gone 100 yards too far.

23   DETWEILER RUN NATURAL AREA

My sense of place was continually distorted as I wandered through Detweiler Run Natural Area in Huntingdon County. Was I really somewhere in New England? Certainly the spring wildflowers that grow there—goldthread, bunchberry, starflower, and Canada mayflower—are common in northern New England's forests. And several of the bird species

Hemlock tree and rhododendron shrubs along Detweiler Run. Detweiler Run Natural Area.

that sing and call and try to lure you away from their nests in early summer—Canada warblers, black-throated blue warblers, and black-throated green warblers—breed more commonly in the North Woods.

Then there are the butterflies—red-spotted purples by the dozen, great-spangled fritillaries, enormous tiger swallowtails, and flashing white admirals. All are temperate species, to be sure, but their numbers, size, and beauty rival those you can see in tropical rainforests. You can also find, among the enormous white oaks growing at Detweiler Run, a tree with a flared base reminiscent of the buttressed tree-trunks of rainforest species.

But then Detweiler Run Natural Area is a patch of Pennsylvania's forest primeval—a remnant of ancient forest, green and spongy with sphagnum moss and dominated by old growth hemlock, white pine, and white oak, with an understory of large rhododendron. The eastern hemlock (*Tsuga canadensis*) is the grandest tree of an eastern North American climax forest. It needs deep shade and moisture to grow, and moves in only after light-loving trees have created a forest. Hemlocks also favor rocks and running water, which Detweiler Run has in abundance. "The hemlock," naturalist Donald Culross Peattie once wrote, "whistles softly to itself. It raises its long, limber boughs and lets them drop again with a sigh, not sorrowful, but letting fall tranquillity upon us."

To reach that tranquil place—a deep ravine between Thickhead and Grass Mountains—you must climb down a steep ridge, following the clearly labeled, orange-blazed Mid State Trail sign through an avenue of moss-covered rocks, mountain laurel, and low-bush blueberries shaded predominately by black gum, wild black cherry, and chestnut oaks of average size. After one-tenth of a mile, you reach the narrow stream valley and turn left, still following the Mid State Trail.

Almost immediately the vegetation changes, with first some large white pine and rhododendron, then hemlock and white oak. Because of a wide buffer zone of mature forest surrounding the official 463-acre natural area, it is difficult to determine where mature forest becomes old growth.

The farther you walk, the more remote the place seems, and the lush mosses muffle even your footsteps. But visitors are never far from the sound of Detweiler Run itself, which is often clogged with debris that creates small falls and rivulets amid banks of sphagnum moss and moldering logs.

Occasionally the monotonous singing of a red-eyed vireo or the cheerful calls of black-capped chickadees reach your ears. If you are especially lucky, you may hit avian paydirt in the dense tangles of rhododendron.

Birds flutter and call and display—brown creepers, ovenbirds, wood thrushes, dark-eyed juncos, and black-and-white, black-throated blue, black-throated green, and Canada warblers are just a few of the deep-woods species that nest there. Other deep-woods species that are present during the breeding season and probably nest there include hooded, worm-eating, and Blackburnian warblers, American redstarts, Louisiana waterthrushes, Acadian flycatchers, scarlet tanagers, veeries, eastern wood pewees, winter wrens, and solitary vireos. Many of these species are difficult to see, but in areas where the trail veers away from the rushing stream waters, you can identify birds by their songs.

The orange-blazed Mid State Trail continues to wind among giant trees and piles of moss-covered rocks. In the midst of the old growth, the blue-blazed Axehandle Trail comes down from the left, so for a shorter circuit (a little more than two miles), climb up that trail to Detweiler Road and turn left back to the parking area.

For a three-mile circuit and a thorough overview of the area, however, continue on the orange-blazed Mid State Trail. Near the end of the natural area, the trail is actually the stony remains of an old railroad bed. At a gas pipeline right-of-way, turn left and climb steeply up along the right-of-way to an old, grass-covered road a short way up the mountainside. Then turn left again and follow the gated Detweiler Road for a level two miles. Be sure to stop and explore a massive rock-slide to the right, a short distance from the right-of-way.

In this area there are no singing warblers. Because the trees are only average-size, the species common to a many-time cutover Pennsylvania woodlot—pleasant, shade-producing, but not awe-inspiring—the bird species are nice to see, but not unusual for this part of Pennsylvania: rufous-sided towhees, tufted titmice, indigo buntings, and rose-breasted grosbeaks, for example.

Of all the pockets of virgin timber in Pennsylvania, Detweiler Run Natural Area stands out as the most glorious, not only for its trees and continual vistas of beauty, but also for its living creatures, the birds and butterflies of an ancient forest.

From State College: Follow U.S. 322 east to Boalsburg. From the traffic light in Boalsburg, continue straight through on Route 322 for 1.9 miles. Turn right on SR 2001. After 0.6 mile, swing right on the main road and continue 0.8 mile until you reach Bear Meadows Road on the left. Follow Bear Meadows Road straight ahead for 3.5 miles, where you take the right fork another 0.1 mile, passing Bear Meadows Natural Area on your right. Continue up and over the next mountain, bearing sharp left 1.6 miles from Bear Meadows at the intersection with Wampler Road. Continue down 0.6 mile to the point where the road makes another hairpin turn to the right. Park on the left near the gate.

24   BIG FLAT LAUREL NATURAL AREA

June is mountain laurel time in Pennsylvania, and what better way is there to celebrate the beauty of the state flower than to explore the Big Flat Laurel Natural Area? Part of Rothrock State Forest on the border of Huntingdon and Centre counties, it is a level plateau atop a 2,400-foot ridge bisected by the orange-blazed Mid State Trail. The trail permits easy access through the 184-acre remote area, which contains a substantial black bear population, the lovely Indian Wells Overlook, the remains of three charcoal flats, and the man-made Keith Springs. But the main attraction is the lush growth of mountain laurel.

Mountain laurel is one of seven shrub species in the genus *Kalmia*, all of which are found only in North America. Named for the eighteenth-century Swedish naturalist Peter Kalm, who spent three years (1748–51) exploring Pennsylvania, New York, New Jersey, and southern Canada in search of hardy plants for his native country, Kalm's journal contains the first detailed accounts of the various *Kalmia* species. About *Kalmia latifolia*, Pennsylvania's mountain laurel, he wrote: "Their beauty rivals that of most of the known trees in nature." The Swedes called them "spoon trees," because Indians made spoons and trowels of the wood, but the English named them "laurel" because their shiny evergreen leaves reminded them of their own unrelated laurel plants. Other local names today are calico-bush, calmoun, spoonwood, and mountain ivy.

In Pennsylvania, mountain laurel often forms dense thickets on mountaintops, with the tall, spreading shrubs rarely exceeding six to eight feet in height. Farther south, members of this species are sometimes the height and breadth of small trees. The present champion, listed by the American Forestry Association, grows 28 feet high with a 47-inch circum-

Mountain laurel in bloom. Big Flat Laurel Natural Area.

ference in Oconee County, South Carolina. The flowers from the southern part of its range, though, are less compact in form, giving the blossoms a scraggly appearance, so for sheer beauty during flowering time, Pennsylvania's mountain laurel, with its thick, umbrella-like clusters of white and pale-pink flowers, far outdoes the southern shrubs.

Both Peter Kalm and another early naturalist, Mark Catesby, mentioned the poisonous leaves of mountain laurel. Young sheep, calves, and goats often died after eating them, and larger livestock were also sickened by it. Today scientists have isolated the chemical that causes the problem—andromedotoxin—and have discovered that it is most lethal to sheep. In fact, the other *Kalmia* common to eastern Pennsylvania, sheep laurel (*Kalmia angustifolia*), contains twice as much poison in its leaves as mountain laurel—hence its nicknames "lambkill" and "sheepkill." Humans too are susceptible to the poison, which is not only in the leaves themselves but also in the honey produced by laurel-pollinating bees.

On the other hand, white-tailed deer have a high tolerance for andromedotoxin and eat mountain laurel leaves during lean winter months. As long as they mix leaves and twigs from other sources in their diet, it does them no harm, and in fact they seem to know just how much they can eat without ill-effects. Not only does mountain laurel provide starvation food for deer, it also provides protection, especially during hunting season, when deer lay up in laurel thickets for days, invisible to all but the most persistent of hunters.

It is the impenetrability of laurel thickets that makes the laurel the bane of mountaintop hikers, as well, which is why the Big Flat Laurel Natural Area is so appealing. Because of the well-maintained Mid State Trail, you can wander easily through the laurel at the height of blossom season and experience the loveliness of a garden planted by nature that is far more satisfying to the senses than a visit to the most spectacular of formal gardens. The peace is broken only by an unending concert of birdsong. Common yellowthroats, black-and-white warblers, rufous-sided towhees, chestnut-sided warblers, and ovenbirds are just a few species that breed in the area.

Although mountain laurel dominates the understory, it grows in company with huckleberry shrubs, bear and chestnut oak, black cherry, red maple, and pitch pine trees. By keeping a close eye on the forest floor, you can also find the delicate flowers of Indian cucumber-root and Canada mayflowers. Spicebush and tiger swallowtail butterflies flutter at eye level, and many of the laurel blossoms are abuzz with bumblebees, their major pollinators.

After walking about three-quarters of a mile on the Mid State Trail, you pass a blue-blazed side trail to your left. Ignore that, and continue on the main trail for another half-mile over the three charcoal flats that are left from nineteenth-century iron operations at nearby Greenwood Furnace. Eventually you reach a large tumble of white boulders overlooking the Bear Meadows Natural Area far below. This is the Indian Wells Overlook, with three wells (actually man-made, rounded depressions in the rocks) at the far end of the boulder area.

Growing between as well as just below the rocks are numerous mountain ash trees, which bloom at the same time as mountain laurel. They have creamy-white, three-to-four-inch-wide flat-topped clusters of blossoms and are just as showy as mountain laurel. In the autumn, bright orange-red clusters of berry-like pomes are equally showy. Known also as American rowantree, winetree, and mountain sumac, its fruit is popular with many species of birds, particularly robins and ruffed grouse. Primarily a northern species, in Pennsylvania it grows either along the borders of cold swamps and bogs or on the rocky mountain ridges, like those at Hawk Mountain Sanctuary and the Big Flat Laurel Natural Area.

Once you have enjoyed the view and puzzled over the "wells" (no one knows who made them or why), return to the blue-blazed side trail and turn right. Near Keith Spring, ferns, chiefly lady and cinnamon, appear in the understory. The spring itself was constructed back in 1934 by the Civilian Conservation Corps, and the water is still good—a cooling place to pause before turning left down the Gettis Ridge Road for the return to your car.

Although mountain laurel always blooms during June, some years are better than others. That is because the seed capsules develop on the flowering clusters after blooming and limit the new-shoot growth, which is necessary for setting flower buds. But whether the year is spectacular for laurel or merely good, the Big Flat Laurel Natural Area is a restful place to spend a day in June when all seems well with the world of nature.

From State College: Follow U.S. 322 east to Boalsburg. At the traffic light in Boalsburg, continue straight through on Route 322 for 1.9 miles. Turn right onto a road with a sign for Tussey Mountain Ski Resort. After 0.6 mile, swing right on the main road and continue 0.8 mile until you reach Bear Meadows Road to the left. Follow Bear Meadows Road straight ahead for 3.5 miles, at which point you turn right on the North Meadows Road and drive approximately 2.5 miles until you reach Gettis Ridge Road. Park there and follow the orange-blazed Mid State Trail north at the point where Gettis Ridge Road joins North Meadows Road.

25   SHAVER'S CREEK ENVIRONMENTAL CENTER

Shaver's Creek Environmental Center is a laboratory facility for Penn State University's School of Hotel, Restaurant, and Recreation Management in the College of Health and Human Development. Located in a portion of the 8,000-acre Stone Valley Recreation Area and University Forest owned by Penn State in Huntingdon County, the center offers a multitude of educational opportunities for both students and visitors.

Students spend many hours every week at Shaver's Creek studying its natural and cultural history, receiving instruction in environmental edu-

Stone Valley Lake. Shaver's Creek Environmental Center.

cation, and designing the displays and exhibits found at the Nature Center building. But because the center also wants to be an active participant in the larger community, membership, a wide variety of interpretive programs, and volunteer positions are open to the general public. On almost any weekend throughout the year, something is going on at Shaver's Creek—an "owl prowl," a winter walk to look for animal tracks, a bird breakfast, maple-sugaring, wildflower walks, moonlight canoeing for two, and so on, and for a small fee anyone, member or nonmember, can participate. One spring-like day in early April, we chose to take a "Lichen Looking" walk with a staff naturalist and seven other people. The naturalist managed to gear the mile-and-a-half walk over Black Walnut Trail to all age levels, so everyone went away a little wiser about lichens and their importance to the natural world. We learned, for instance, that there are 15,000 species of lichens worldwide and that most are difficult to identify without a microscope and chemical testing. Lichens are excellent indicators of pollution. They grow better in the winter than in the summer, although that growth is a mere 1 to 10 millimeters a year. Lichens can be divided into three groups by any amateur observer. Crustose lichens look like discolored patches on rocks and may be why the word "lichen" means "leprous" in Greek, leafy-looking lichens belong to the foliose group, and branching lichens (such as "reindeer moss," which is really a lichen) are in the fruticose group.

Once we started looking for lichens we found them everywhere, on trees and rocks, dead branches, moss beds, and in every conceivable color—red, yellow, green, blue, black, orange, and brown. Most of us could positively identify only one lichen species, the red-tipped British soldiers' lichen, but in a moist, flat area along the Black Walnut Trail we found not only that species but also a host of other representatives from each of the three groups. As with any good naturalist-led walk, trees, birds, wildflowers, and mosses were pointed out in passing.

For 17 years Shaver's Creek had a Bird of Prey Rehabilitation Facility that took in, fed, and cared for injured raptors. It raised money from concerned citizens to operate the facility, but long-term care is expensive, especially for birds that can never be released because of permanent handicaps. Such birds—and there were several—were socialized by volunteers so they could be used in their "Traveling Raptor Show," which goes to schools and meetings of local community groups in the Central Pennsylvania area.

Recently, because of funding shortages, Shaver's Creek personnel stopped rehabilitating nonendangered raptors, referring such birds to other state-licensed rehabilitators. But state-of-the-art flight cages containing endangered raptors still attract visitors, who learn why those birds are there in the first place. Most have been hit by cars, caught in traps, or shot.

Another favorite bird-watching place is inside the center's lecture room in front of a large window that looks out on bird feeders of all sizes and shapes filled with sunflower and thistle seeds. There you can see Carolina wrens, purple finches, and eastern goldfinches, as well as the more common species, such as dark-eyed juncos, black-capped chickadees, tufted titmice, and red-bellied, hairy, and downy woodpeckers. Red and gray squirrels are also abundant.

To see wildlife along the 25 miles of trails that wind through deep woodlands, across open hillsides, and beside streams and cattail marshes, including a boardwalk near the center, it is best to purchase a trail map at the center for a nominal cost. The map shows such trails as the 4-mile-long Shaver's Creek Trail, the 2½-mile Homestead Trail, and the 12-and-a-half-mile Iron Stone Trail.

One of the easiest and most interesting trails, especially during waterfowl migration, is the circular two-and-a-half-mile Lake Trail. The 72-acre Stone Valley Lake was created in 1960 by damming Shaver's Creek for recreation purposes. Some of the waterfowl species you might see there are buffleheads, horned grebes, common loons, lesser scaups, and common mergansers. Another interesting and educational trail is the Woodcock Management Demonstration Area and Trail, which was designed by the School of Forest Resources in the adjacent Stone Valley Experimental Forest. An excellent trail guide is available free from Penn State's College of Agricultural Sciences. This area is being managed to provide American woodcock with habitat requirements for breeding, nesting, and migration. The trail of less than a mile is orange-blazed and includes courtship singing grounds for woodcocks in March and April, and nesting cover.

Altogether, the Shaver's Creek Environmental Center and adjacent Stone Valley Recreation Area and Experimental Forest provide many opportunities to learn more about the natural world from enthusiastic professionals and to learn on your own by exploring the diverse trails and ecosystems in this beautiful Central Pennsylvania valley.

For more information about the center and its programs, call 814-863-2000 or 814-667-3424. For a fee, anyone can become a member for and receive both a seasonal program guide and Shavings, *the seasonal newsletter.*

From State College: Take Pa. 26 to Pine Grove Mills. At the blinking light, turn left, still on Route 26. After 4 miles, turn right at the sign for Stone Valley Recreation Area and Shaver's Creek Environmental Center. Drive 1.7 miles and turn left at sign for Shaver's Creek. (Shortly before you reach this area is the sign for the Woodcock Trail on your left.) After 0.3 mile, bear right into Shaver's Creek and park.

26   ROCKY RIDGE NATURAL AREA

Rocky Ridge Natural Area is noted both for its rock formations and for its diversity of wildflowers. Located in Rothrock State Forest in Huntingdon County, this 150-acre tract is especially attractive during May at the height

Flowering dogwood tree blossoms and rock outcroppings. Rocky Ridge
Natural Area.

of spring wildflowers. If you are a wildflower enthusiast, you will hardly
notice the steep, 300-foot climb from Frew Road to the top of Rocky Ridge
following the orange-blazed Link Trail, because you will be so engrossed
in identifying the wildflowers that blanket the slope—trout-lilies, skunk
cabbage, kidney-leaved buttercups, mayapples, wild geranium, golden
ragwort, spring beauties, rue anemones, wild ginger, sessile and perfoliate bellworts, round-leaved hepaticas, squawroot, black cohosh, Solomon's seal, round-leaved pyrola, both pink and yellow lady's slippers,
showy orchis, yellow mandarin, and mitrewort, to name only a few.

When you reach the ridgetop, you might also be able to spot the single
large leaf of the rare-to-Pennsylvania puttyroot orchid, *Aplectrum hyemale*.
This leaf develops in the summer, lasts through the winter, and then with-
ers before the yellowish, greenish, or whitish flowers bloom on the single
10- to 16-inch stalk in June. It prefers a moist soil and is spotty in its
distribution in Pennsylvania.

But the other rare-to-Pennsylvania wildflower, *Obolaria virginica* or pennywort, with its clusters of white flowers on a six-inch-high stem, will be
in bloom. A member of the gentian family, pennywort is the only species
of *Obolaria* in the world, and its scientific name comes from the obolos, a

Greek coin much like our penny, in a reference to the plant's round leaves. Its range is wide—from New Jersey to Illinois, and south to Florida and Texas in moist woods—but, like puttyroot, its distribution in Pennsylvania is sparse. The existence of these two uncommon species in the natural area, as well as the sheer diversity of wildflowers (58 and still counting), accounts for Rocky Ridge's botanical reputation.

Take the trail to the left along the ridgetop to see looming rock formations of Oriskany sandstone. According to geologist Robert H. Washburn, "the sandstone outcrop forming the crest of Rocky Ridge is unique from both a geologic and scenic standpoint." Although nearby Jacks Mountain and Warrior Ridge are composed of the same sandstone, most of it has been quarried for the manufacture of glass and abrasives. On Rocky Ridge the boulders have been allowed to stand as rocky sentinels, "a sculpture garden . . . of towering, water-scoured boulders, . . . pockmarked monoliths, twisted and jumbled . . . like the backbone of a reclining giant," as Jean Aron, author of *The Short Hiker,* describes it. Because the Oriskany sandstone is resistant to weathering, it forms great boulders that over eons of time are dislodged and displaced into the fantastic formations found on the ridge.

One hundred feet below the boulders are limestone sinkholes whose density, number, and close spacing on a ridgetop are unusual. Washburn maintains that it is "because of the unique geology, steeply dipping rock layers of limestone and sandstone, [that] there is a unique botanical habitat."

Those boulders are a drawing card for visitors—young and old alike—to climb and to examine the ebony spleenwort and common polypody ferns growing on them. Other ferns in the natural area include maidenhair, rattlesnake, and Christmas ferns. Ant lion activity in the sand beneath the rocks is also interesting to watch. Look for small depressions or pits in the sand made by ant lions, insects that eat ants when they slip down the pits into the jaws of the hidden, waiting ant lions.

For bird-watchers, there is a wide variety of woodland species. When we visited we found a mourning dove nest of white pine needles and sticks containing two eggs on top of one large rock—a somewhat unusual place for a mourning dove to build. Mourning doves usually prefer to construct loose platforms of twigs in tree crotches or vines, and on rail fences or stumps. Only where trees are scarce do they nest on the ground, on house-roof gutters, in chimney corners, or on the tops of numerous songbird nests. In Pennsylvania they are more likely to be found in the suburbs or in farmyards. But apparently at least one mourning dove pair prefers the wilds of Rocky Ridge and the security of the large, hidden-from-view rock to raise their family.

Other birds to look and listen for include pileated, hairy, and red-bellied woodpeckers, solitary vireos, scarlet tanagers, golden-crowned kinglets, Louisiana waterthrushes, eastern phoebes, ruffed grouse, and wild turkeys.

After thoroughly exploring the ridgetop, continue left on the trail. Once you reach the powerline right-of-way, you have left the natural area and you can either turn left and follow the right-of-way down to the road, or continue following the orange-blazed Link Trail through the newly designated "special management" area of the state forest adjacent to the natural area. That trail eventually winds its way off the ridge and crosses Frew Road. Along the way, you will find still more wildflowers. Then turn left onto the road and follow it back to the parking area, still watching for wildflowers along the edges of the road. No matter where you walk in May on Rocky Ridge, it is a flowery paradise, so take along a wildflower guide and spend the day.

From State College: Follow Pa. 26 south to Pine Grove Mills. At the light, turn left, still on 26, and drive 9.2 miles to stop sign in McAlevy's Fort. Turn right on Route 26 south, and then left after 0.9 mile. Continue for 4.1 miles on Route 26 and then turn left onto Martin Gap Road. (You will see a Martin Gap sign on your left after you turn.) After driving 1.0 miles, cross a bridge and turn right onto a dirt road. Follow the dirt road into Rothrock State Forest, passing a shale pit and two cabins. When the road forks, 0.9 mile from the bridge, keep right and follow Frew Road for half a mile. Park at the gated road on the left where the orange-blazed Link Trail crosses Frew Road. Follow the trail across the road, down over the stream, and up Rocky Ridge.

27   FRANK E. MASLAND JR. NATURAL AREA

The 1,270-acre Frank E. Masland Jr. Natural Area, part of the Tuscarora State Forest in Perry County, contains the finest oak forest in the state.

Laurel Run. Frank E. Masland Jr. Natural Area.

This section of the Appalachian Mountains Ridge-and-Valley province includes a portion of two ridges: Bowers Mountain (1,921 feet) and Middle Ridge (1,700 feet). Tucked between the parallel ridges in classic Ridge-and-Valley topography is a stream-cut valley formed by the North Branch of Laurel Run, which flows at an elevation of 1,150 feet.

In winter and summer you will probably find yourself alone and hear no human-induced sounds but those of an occasional airplane. However, a winter visit, in late January, is possible only if you have four-wheel drive, especially for the ascent of Middle Ridge on Laurel Run Road. But what a way to buoy winter-weary spirits! Vistas are open, making it easy to see deer and birds, and what you can't see, you will find recorded in the snow. Along the trails, deer, squirrel, and fox tracks are abundant. Dead trees are riddled with pileated woodpecker holes, and fresh pieces of bark on the snow provide evidence that at least one is in residence.

Tree persons will also enjoy a winter visit because both living and fallen giants appear more impressive without their leaves. Despite heavy cutting on the ridge for tannin extraction, and partial cutting along the stream bottom during the last century, many old-growth trees 32 to 40 inches in diameter at breast height and over 100 feet tall are common—hemlock, red, black, scarlet, chestnut, and white oak, yellow poplar, black gum, red maple, and a few white pine—especially along the stream valley. Because of the thinner, drier soils, the same trees near the top of the ridge are only half as high (50 feet) as those growing in the richer soil near the stream. Sold to the commonwealth as part of the Pennsylvania Forest Reserve in 1907, the only cutting done on the tract since then was during the 1930s, when the Civilian Conservation Corps cut dead American chestnut snags along the roads and trails.

After descending steadily downward on the Turbett Trail for more than a mile, you will reach the ice-and-snow-clogged Laurel Run, lined with hemlocks and large white oaks. The focal point, though, is a massive white pine tree overhanging the water. Luckily the stream valley is wide, so it is easy to pick your way upstream over dry land in search of Deer Hollow Trail. In winter it is also relatively simple to bushwack upstream to where the hollow comes down. You may or may not hit the official trail back up the ridge, but with the bare bones of the landscape exposed and the Ridge-and-Valley province so geometrically evident, you can continue up the ridge until you reach the road. Turn left and follow it back to the parking area.

The largest tree in the natural area, a yellow poplar 41 inches in diameter and 120 feet high, grows on the north side of Deer Hollow Trail, so be on the lookout for it, as well as for several giant oak trees. A few winter birds to look for are golden-crowned kinglets, black-capped chickadees, and ruffed grouse. Altogether, you will have walked two and a half miles on that circuit.

How different the Frank E. Masland Jr. Natural Area is on a hot, humid August day, but the giant trees along Laurel Run provide a cool refuge, so enter the tract at the Phoenix Bridge Access Point. Dark and shaded, for the most part, only the occasional tree fall lets in sunbursts of light.

Rock-hopping back and forth over Laurel Run, often across large, flat ledges barely under water, is part of the fun. So is watching the native brook trout darting about in the deep pools of this Wilderness Trout Stream, so designated by the Pennsylvania Fish and Boat Commission. A large rock outcropping on the right side of Laurel Run has common polypody ferns sprouting from its crevices, but the only summer wildflowers are Indian pipes growing in the wet leaf duff near the stream.

The farther in you walk, the larger the trees become, particularly the hemlocks and white oaks. After a mile of pleasant meandering, following a network of animal and human trails, you will reach the lower end of Deer Hollow Trail. Then retrace your steps back to your car. Or, if you want to see what the winter hike looks like in summer, hike that same circuit. Be forewarned, however, that the gnats are fierce and the trails are overgrown in places.

Named for carpet manufacturer and outstanding conservationist Frank E. Masland Jr. of Carlisle, the natural area is an excellent example of what a mature Pennsylvania forest should look like. This is now a rare sight in a state where most landowners, both public and private, continue to "harvest" trees as soon as they reach 11 inches in diameter. This not only diminishes the productivity and diversity of the woods, but also makes them hotter and drier on sultry summer days.

From Carlisle: Follow Pa. 74 north 13 miles to the village of Bridgeport. Turn left at the sign to Landisburg. Go 1 mile and turn left again at the center of Landisburg on Pa. 233 west (sign indicates Newville, 17 miles). Drive 3.5 miles and bear right off the highway on Laurel Run Road. Drive 10 miles on that road, which changes from paved into gravel, turn right, and go 0.3 mile up a hill to the entrance to the Turbett Trail on the right. Deer Hollow Trail is to the right, 0.2 mile farther, and the Phoenix Bridge Access Point is 0.6 mile beyond that, at the bottom of the hill.

28 HEMLOCKS NATURAL AREA

Shafts of sunlight beamed through the dense virgin hemlock canopy during our early August visit to the Hemlocks Natural Area. This 120-acre tract, part of the Tuscarora State Forest in Perry County, memorializes the now nearly extinct, original white pine/hemlock forests of Pennsylvania.

Of all the remnant virgin tracts we have visited in the commonwealth, the Hemlocks Natural Area seems to have the most large trees and regeneration of seedlings. According to the Pennsylvania Bureau of Forestry, more than half the hemlock trees are at least 24 inches in diameter at four and a half feet above ground, the largest has a diameter of 51 inches, the tallest is 123 feet high, and the average age of the trees is between 300 and 500 years old.

Patterson Run. Hemlocks Natural Area.

During our first visit to the area in 1977, four years after it was declared a Registered Natural Landmark, we ambled along its northeastern section. Following no discernible path, and rock-hopping frequently back and forth across Patterson Run, we searched for level footing in the narrow stream valley. Woodland ferns blanket the steep-sided, boulder-strewn slopes. Those slopes are a deterrent now to white-tailed deer predation on tree seedlings, just as they were to loggers between 1880 and 1891, when most of the rest of Perry County was lumbered off. As a result, massive living trees tower over the moldering, moss-covered trunks of fallen giants undisturbed by human management. Above the rushing mountain stream, only the haunting strains of wood thrush music, occasional raucous cries of blue jays, alarm chirps of chipmunks, and long-winded sermons from the "preacher bird" or red-eyed vireo are audible.

When we returned to the Hemlocks Natural Area many years later, we drove to the southeast end to park and walk a portion of the much-improved three-mile trail network encircling it. As visitors descend the steep path from the parking lot in August, they will be welcomed by the contrasting excitable "yank-yanks" of white-breasted nuthatches and the lazy, drawling "pee-a-wees" of the eastern wood pewees.

To the left of the trail, the first of the large eastern hemlocks towers. Designated Pennsylvania's official tree by Act 233 of the Pennsylvania Legislature on June 21, 1931, it is also known as the Canadian hemlock because of its scientific name *Tsuga canadensis*. But although it ranges from Nova Scotia to the north shore of Lake Huron in Canada, its widest distribution is in the eastern United States west of the Coastal Plain. Donald Culross Peattie, in his classic and informative *A Natural History of Trees of Eastern and Central North America*, once wrote: "In the grand, high places of the southern mountains Hemlock soars above the rest of the forest, rising like a church spire—like numberless spires as far as the eye can see—through the blue haze that is the natural atmosphere of those ranges."

Pennsylvania once had similar ranks of magnificent old hemlock, but early settlers quickly learned from Native Americans about the curative uses of its bark. High in tannin, it helps to heal burns and sores. Then they discovered that it also tans leather a beautiful shade of red. Usually they cut the trees, stripped their bark, and left the logs to rot in the forest. Today it is primarily used for rough lumber, building construction, and boxes and crates, and as pulpwood—but, again in Peattie's words, "not in newsprint and cheap wrapping paper does Hemlock serve us best, but rather rooted in its tranquil, age-old stations."

Tranquillity is what the Hemlocks Natural Area offers those who seek it, along with a scenic mountain stream studded with small waterfalls that is at the base of the descent from the parking lot. When you reach the stream, turn left on Hemlock Trail, watching for beds of spongy sphagnum moss and several soon-to-be-open whorled wood asters. Stop frequently to sit on boulders beside Patterson Run and you may spot a native brook trout slipping through a deep pool.

This is also a good place to find butterflies—tiger swallowtails, spring azures, and great-spangled fritillaries, all of which add life and color to the understory. The larvae of great-spangled fritillaries feed on violets in the springtime, and there are remnants of several violet species, as well as the leaves of the woods-loving starflowers, along the trail.

Higher in the trees, black-capped chickadees, both hairy and downy woodpeckers, the omnipresent red-eyed vireos, American redstarts, and even Blackburnian warblers might be seen or heard. Especially wonderful to see is the male Blackburnian warbler, his flaming orange head and throat setting off his black-and-white back and breast. Known also as the "hemlock warbler," Blackburnian warblers traditionally prefer to nest high in the dense canopy provided by mature hemlock forests, although they will nest in mature deciduous woodlands too. According to the *Atlas of Breeding Birds in Pennsylvania*, Blackburnian warblers have been confirmed as breeders in the Hemlocks Natural Area.

Another breeding bird, which scolds constantly, is the stream-loving Louisiana waterthrush. A so-called aberrant warbler that both looks and acts more like a wood thrush than a warbler, it skulks in the underbrush, its brown-and-white body blending with the leaf duff. But when it forages on a low-hanging branch or walks along the stream edge on its long, pale-pink legs, it frequently pauses to slowly pump its tail up and down like a spotted sandpiper, earning it the nicknames "wagtail," "wagtail warbler," and "water wagtail." This bird builds a well-hidden nest tucked into a stream bank or under tree roots. Best of all, its loud, ringing calls in rushing mountain stream ravines are usually one of the first signs of spring, since it returns to Pennsylvania as early as the first week in April.

On either side of the trail, hemlock seedlings sprout thickly on the forest floor or on fallen hemlock tree trunks. On these nurse-tree trunks the seedlings usually grow in a relatively straight line. In several places straight lines of mature hemlocks march down one slope and up the other, as if they too had once sprouted on decaying logs. Mixed in with the hemlocks are predominantly black and yellow birch trees, along with a scattering of red and chestnut oaks and red maples.

What with the butterflies and birds, wildflowers and trees, and the overall ambience of the place, it may take a couple of hours to cover the less-than-a-mile-long Hemlock Trail. Eventually, however, you will cross a wooden bridge and angle left up the hillside on the Laurel Trail until you reach the Rim Trail. Turn right and head back toward the parking lot. That trail runs high above the stream valley and the hemlock trees and presents an overview of the natural area. Finally it intersects with the Hemlock Trail, which leads across Patterson Run on another bridge. Take a short right and you will reach the steep climb back up to the parking lot.

After so many tranquil hours, it is difficult to reenter the "real" world. To me, the Hemlocks Natural Area evokes William Butler Yeats's "The Lake Isle of Innisfree," with its "bee-loud glade," where "I shall have some peace there, for peace comes dropping slow." Like Yeats, "While I stand on the roadway, or on the pavements gray, I hear it in the deep heart's core." But instead of an Irish lake at Innisfree, I recall the abiding peace of a remnant ancient forest in Pennsylvania.

From Exit 14 of the Pennsylvania Turnpike (Willow Hill): Turn left, north, on Pa. 75. Follow Route 75 for 10.9 miles and bear right, just beyond the village of

Doylesburg, onto Pa. 274 east toward New Germantown. After 4.8 miles, turn right on Hemlock Road. Enter the Hemlocks Natural Area 2.2 miles farther, but then continue another 1.6 miles to the parking area on the left.

29   WAGGONER'S GAP

On any crisp, windy autumn day, thousands of people head for *the* world-renowned Hawk Mountain Sanctuary. Located atop Kittatinny Ridge in Berks and Schuylkill counties, it offers a panoramic view of migrating raptors. Increasingly, though, hawk watchers are seeking out other, less-crowded ridges and discovering, by keeping sophisticated records, that *any* ridge in Pennsylvania may offer spectacular raptor sightings.

Such a place is 1,476-foot-high Waggoner's Gap just off Route 74, eight miles north of Carlisle at the crest of Blue Mountain. Blue Mountain is the local name of the same Kittatinny Ridge of Hawk Mountain fame.

As the hawk flies, Waggoner's Gap is about 70 miles southwest of Hawk Mountain, yet its yearly raptor tally differs from that of the latter. For instance, in 1987 "Waggoner's Gap had the best season for any hawk watch with over 30,000 birds," according to Gregory Smith, Northern Appalachian Regional Editor for the Hawk Migration Association of America. Furthermore, Smith says, "Waggoner's is the number one spot for golden eagles east of the Rocky Mountains." In 1993, observers counted a record 132 golden eagles there, 75 of which appeared in November. In that month, the best time is the second week.

So, on a cold, clear November morning try to get to Waggoner's Gap as early as possible and you will be introduced to a whole new vocabulary: hard-core, hawk-watcher language. People sit on a huge jumble of tilted, flat-sided, north-facing boulders and announce each bird as it approaches. In addition to golden eagles, you should see a lot of "tails." "Tails," in hawkese, means red-tailed hawks. "T.V.'s" (turkey vultures) are also fairly common, but "shoulders" (red-shouldered hawks) are scarce.

Raptor watchers. Waggoner's Gap.

In addition to interpreting the abbreviated bird names, you also have to figure out where to look for the raptors someone always spots long before you will. "Over seventy-four" translates as "over Route 74," where it crosses Tuscarora Ridge to the northwest of Blue Mountain, and "over dead stuff" means coming down Blue Mountain straight toward spectators and sailing above a large, dead tree.

Several groups form and re-form during a day on the ridge as people come and go and are hailed by friends already occupying their favorite rocks. The core group coalesces around whoever is counting for the official records. In 1990, for the first time, Waggoner's Gap was manned from the first of August until the first of December. This full coverage later amounted to 796 hours by December, and during most of those hours volunteer counters were there no matter what the weather conditions.

Although golden eagles are the big drawing card, the first two weeks in November are also a peak time for red-tailed hawks. Mid-September is prime time for broad-winged hawks, late August and September for bald eagles, and October for sharp-shinned hawks. But the best time to see the greatest diversity of raptor species is during the first two weeks in October.

On October 7, 1990, for instance, 13 species were recorded including 49 ospreys, 601 sharp-shinned hawks, 31 Cooper's hawks, 12 northern harriers, 4 northern goshawks, and 2 peregrine falcons. That same year, four new station records were set—osprey 585, American kestrel 377, merlin 43, and peregrine falcon 51—with an overall count of 16,160 raptors. No wonder Waggoner's Gap is gaining more renown each year in hawk-watching circles.

But you don't have to be a raptor expert to enjoy a day of hawk-watching. Even on Hawk Mountain, experts share what they know with novices. All you need to do is sit tight and listen. In fact, one of the best features of hawk-watching is the sense of camaraderie among the participants. The small, congenial group at Waggoner's Gap engages in a good deal of socializing, so even on slow days there is no chance for boredom. On the day we visited, several people were passing around photographs they had taken of birds of prey, and one man even shared his videotape of raptors. They reminded me of proud grandparents exchanging photos of precious grandchildren.

Such distractions, though, do not deter hawk-watchers from the business at hand. Because the valleys are wide on either side of the ridge, and many of the birds of prey fly over them instead of over the mountaintop, super eyes are sometimes needed to make positive identifications. And there is almost always someone who has a spotting scope. Often, the first spotter will call out his or her guess, then the others will debate the identification, discussing aloud what they think it might be and why until they reach a general consensus or until the bird in question obliges by coming in for a close look.

Luckily for us, golden eagles found the rocky ridgetop alluring, and at 12:21 P.M. we saw our first golden eagle flying, in tandem, with a common raven. Or was the raven merely ushering the eagle through its territory? With binoculars we had an excellent view of the golden eagle as it flew past. Everyone cheered! The second golden eagle we saw, at 1:04 P.M., was not ushered through, but rather chased by two common ravens directly overhead, too close even for binoculars. Such thrills only fuel the ardor of hawk-watchers.

Caution: The rocks are treacherous. Some of the volunteers have even taken nasty falls. Be sure to wear rubber-soled hiking boots with good traction on rocks. A comfortable pillow, a picnic lunch and beverage, and, on sunny days, sunblock, are highly recommended. And don't forget your binoculars!

From Carlisle: Take Pa. 74 north for 8 miles until you reach the top of Blue Mountain. Pull into one of the parking areas on either side of the road and walk a few hundred feet up the hill on the right to the rock outcropping, which is the main lookout.

30   HOLLY GAP PRESERVE

The 913-acre Holly Gap Preserve in Mt. Holly Springs, Cumberland County, is a mini-wilderness from its open sedge meadow/marsh and seepage swamp area deep in water and muck, to its more typical Central Pennsylvania upland forest environment.

Back in 1987, acting on old 1950s records indicating that the preserve area harbored the state-endangered bog turtle, the Pennsylvania Chapter of The Nature Conservancy reconfirmed the population during the spring. But in the process of poking around they discovered an even more endangered species, the globally rare plant glade or purple-flowered spurge (*Euphorbia pupurea*). First discovered in a mountain glade in Pennsylvania in 1838 by the flamboyant botanist Rafinesque, today it is found on less than 30 sites worldwide in West Virginia, Virginia, and North Carolina, in addition to Pennsylvania. At Holly Gap Preserve the plant lives in the forested seepage swamp, an area thick with skunk cabbage and sphagnum moss species, not to mention an understory of poison sumac, spicebush, and holly overtopped by a canopy of red maple, black ash, and hemlock.

With the help of a local guide, we found the glade spurge hidden in the thick underbrush when we visited in September. But without their tiny deep-purple, cup-shaped flowers, the plants appear as unprepossessing as the rest of the area. Yet we felt a certain reverence as we looked at the rare plant—the stuff of botanists' dreams—even though to most people the forested seepage swamp is a nightmare in summer. Then it is thick with mosquitoes, and northern copperhead snakes are common—reason enough, scientists hope, to keep both the glade spurge and bog turtles safe from collectors.

The bog turtle is an especially engaging creature, small enough (four inches) to fit perfectly into a youngster's hand, and as a result greatly

Mountain Creek. Holly Gap Preserve.

sought after by some people in the pet trade and by the unscrupulous collectors who still try to supply them. Ignorant collectors—people who see them and take them home as they would the common box or painted turtles, not knowing the difference—are also a problem. Thus, the location of the refuge with the largest known population of bog turtles in the world—the Acopian Preserve in Lancaster County—is a scientific secret. It was there, accompanied by a Conservancy biologist, that I had seen my only bog turtle.

The bog turtles at the Holly Gap Preserve are even more elusive. Although it appears that the turtles utilize a large portion of both the open marsh/meadow and the forested seepage swamp at various times of the year, ongoing studies should make more sense of the life history of bog turtles, both at Holly Gap Preserve and at the Acopian Preserve.

Like many endangered species, much more needs to be learned about bog turtles to safeguard them for future generations. For instance, scientists do not know why one site attracts bog turtles and another, which appears identical, has none. All they know is that bog turtles live in sunny, humid sphagnum bogs, swamps, or marshy meadows containing soft-bottomed, meandering streams anywhere from sea level in New Jersey to 4,200 feet in the Appalachian Mountains of western North Carolina.

Also known as Muhlenberg's turtle (*Clemmys muhlenbergii*), after the early Pennsylvania naturalist/Lutheran minister who first discovered it in the late eighteenth century in Lancaster County, it was the first turtle species put on Pennsylvania's endangered species list back in 1977. Loss of boggy habitat has been the other reason for its decline, so it is particularly important to save the known areas they still utilize.

Most visitors to the Holly Gap Preserve pull into the parking lot just off Route 94 on Ridge Road and follow the path winding along Mountain Creek for several miles, content to view the open marsh and seepage swamp from a distance. The 200-acre wetland contains spotted, painted, snapping, and stinkpot turtles, in addition to the bog turtle. When the water is high, it attracts such waterfowl as Canada geese, mallards, and wood ducks. Other wetland bird species include great blue herons, belted kingfishers, and green-backed herons. Muskrats and mink, ruffed grouse and American woodcock, and barred, screech, and great horned owls are also abundant.

At the beginning of the trail you can see the remnants of an old dam destroyed by the Pennsylvania Fish and Boat Commission eight years ago so the artificial lake could revert to a wetland. Along the wide trail, a former logging road, look for several huge virgin white pines. Bottled gentian, a fall-blooming wildflower, provides a beautiful contrast to the scarlet-clustered berries of jack-in-the-pulpit. The elegant royal fern is the showiest of the ferns inhabiting the wet areas, while the most dominant marsh shrub is high-bush blueberry, which thrives in a sea of sedges and cattails. Nodding ladies'-tresses, a late-blooming member of the Orchid family, grows in the boggy meadows.

Because of the endangered species in the open sedge meadow/marsh and forested seepage swamp, The Nature Conservancy decided that that area should be off-limits to hunting and fishing and other use-oriented disturbances. Fishing is allowed along certain designated points on Mountain Creek, and hunting on the 700-plus acres of remaining preserve where wild turkey and white-tailed deer thrive.

The Nature Conservancy, together with the local people, raised the money to purchase Holly Gap Preserve. Unlike most land-acquisition projects, which depend on big donations from foundations, corporations, and wealthy individuals, $300,000 of the purchase price came from average citizens in small donations.

In addition, the Cumberland County Commissioners, along with the Conservancy, obtained $200,000 from the Pennsylvania Department of Community Affairs Recreation Improvement and Rehabilitation Act

Grant program, and the Commissioners pledged an additional $10,000 on behalf of the county. Another $10,000 came from the Pennsylvania Legislative Initiative Program through the efforts of the local state representative. All this effort was orchestrated by The Nature Conservancy in concert with a local Holly Gap Committee and was one of the largest grassroots land-acquisition efforts ever launched in the commonwealth.

On Saturday, June 27, 1992, Conservancy staff and volunteers and Cumberland County officials dedicated Holly Gap Preserve with a celebration and nature walks attended by 70 local residents. Although the entire preserve was donated by the Conservancy to Cumberland County, the Conservancy will continue to manage the 200-acre marsh of the preserve to protect the rare species.

It is obvious to visitors that the Holly Gap Preserve is a special place, offering refuge not only to endangered species but also to humans who like to hike, fish, hunt, or just appreciate, and it will remain a place of solace and inspiration for many years to come.

From Exit 14 off Interstate 81 on the southern outskirts of Carlisle: Follow Pa. 34 south 5 miles to Mount Holly Springs. Proceed on Route 34 through the town, 0.3 mile beyond the end of the main street. Turn right on Ridge Road just beyond the Deer Lodge Restaurant, a log structure on the right. Drive 0.3 mile on the gravel road next to the stream, and park in the parking area on the left.

31   GETTYSBURG NATIONAL MILITARY PARK

For those of you who would like to combine a little history with wildlife-watching, consider visiting Gettysburg National Military Park in the winter. You will not only see the site of the bloodiest, most decisive battle of the Civil War, but also be able to watch hundreds of black and turkey vultures soar overhead. That is because Gettysburg contains the northernmost winter roosting site for vultures in North America.

Until the Resource Management Specialist for the park began asking

Black vultures. Gettysburg National Military Park.

questions about the large Gettysburg vulture population, some people believed that the present-day vultures were the very same birds that had arrived after the battle in 1863 to clean up the dead horses. But the average life-span of a vulture is between 30 and 40 years. Furthermore, turkey vultures were in the area long before the battle, probably encouraged by farmstead-clearing as early as 1750. Black vultures, on the other hand, are primarily a southern species and did not emigrate north of the Mason-Dixon Line until the late 1930s or the early 1940s.

Although folklore about the birds was easily discounted, scientific reasons for why Gettysburg is popular today with both species of vultures were scarce. So biologists launched studies of roost characteristics and the courting, nesting, and feeding behavior of both turkey vultures and black vultures. They discovered that the protected park and its environs provide excellent roosting habitat for vultures, as well as a surplus of food and nesting sites.

The center of vulture activity is, coincidentally, focused on an area nicknamed "The Valley of Death," after the battle. Just below Big Round Top, in a mixed-hardwood and white-pine forest, is the winter roost site. Directly north of Devil's Den on an open, rock-strewn hillside called Houck's Ridge, as well as at Granite Farm, are so-called "staging areas" where vultures go to bask in the rising sun. They wait there for proper air thermals to form so they can soar off to feed on both domestic and wild carrion. And in the spring they nest among the enormous boulders on Big Round Top, Devil's Den below, and nearby Granite Farm.

During the daytime, as soon as you approach the area you will notice vultures circling overhead. If you are especially observant you will be able to distinguish the chunkier, short-tailed black vultures with their white-tipped wings from the longer-tailed, more graceful turkey vultures. But coming from an area that has only turkey vultures, as I do, I found it easier to tell them apart close up. Black vultures, which are bolder and more aggressive than turkey vultures, are uniformly black-bodied with naked, gray faces that remind me of squirrel monkeys. Turkey vultures have a good deal of brown on the backs of their dark wings and backs, and their heads are red.

The best time to visit is a cold day in January or February. During our visit on a windy day in late January, I was able to study both species closely after we climbed the path to the top of Big Round Top in the midst of a snow flurry. A slight rustling sound alerted us to the presence of 80 vultures crowded onto the branches of several deciduous trees as they waited out the squall. They were mostly turkey vultures, half of which took off as soon as the weather cleared, but enough of both species remained seated at eye level, so I could easily tell them apart without my binoculars.

The turkey vultures spread their wings to bask in the sunlight like anhingas, while the black vultures maintained the classic hunched-up vulture position. For more than an hour they alternately preened, soared from tree to tree, and basked, all in total silence.

If you want to see the roost area, walk slowly and silently along the path at the base of Big Round Top, directly across the stream from Devil's Den, in either late afternoon or early morning, find a white pine with whitewash beneath, and sit down nearby. There you can watch them enter the roost at dusk or leave the roost at first light. If you arrive in the morning before dawn and have the patience to wait awhile, you will see hundreds of vultures streaming from the protection of the pines toward Houck's Ridge.

Then drive along the Auto Tour road between Devil's Den and the Wheatfield, stopping below the ridge. Vultures are perched in hardwood and white pine trees on the ridgetop, stacked up along the fence rails, and parading around the field with the cattle. As the sun rises over Little Round Top, the vultures seem to glow from within.

Suddenly the stereotype of ugly vultures is banished and other adjectives descriptive of vultures come to mind. "Comical" seems more suitable as they stalk around on the ground, heads thrust down and forward, resembling belligerent bullies at a local playground. If they land in the pasture beside your car for a closer look, they may even seem endearing. But they are definitely imposing as they perch in regal splendor, shining in the sunlight. Finally, as they float effortlessly off into the sky, they are both graceful and beautiful. Animated, warm-blooded life in the midst of a battlefield dedicated to death, the vultures of Gettysburg are fitting residents of the former blood-soaked site.

From York: Follow U.S. 30 west to Gettysburg. In the center of town, turn left onto Washington Street and drive 0.5 mile to the intersection with Steinwehr Avenue. Continue straight ahead on Taneytown Road about 0.2 mile to the Visitor Center, to pick up a map of the battlefield, which will outline the Auto Tour that will take you to the area of Little and Big Round Top, Devil's Den, Houck's Ridge, and the Wheatfield.

32 SWEET ROOT NATURAL AREA

Imagine a hot, humid day in late summer. Then imagine walking into a cool virgin forest so remote that all you will hear is the singing of birds and the low mutter of flowing water. Such a place is the Sweet Root Natural Area in Bedford County. One of thirteen pockets of old-growth timber left in Pennsylvania after the clear-cut logging of the nineteenth and early twentieth centuries, this forested water gap was protected, along with the other virgin timber remnants, as a Forest Monument back in 1921.

The original tract consisted of 69 acres of virgin hemlock and cove hardwood along Sweet Root Run hemmed in by 100-foot-high cliffs of Tuscarora sandstone on one side and a steep ridge on the other. Then, in 1971, as part of Buchanan State Forest, the surrounding watershed as well as the virgin pocket were included in the newly designated 1,400-acre

Sweet Root Run. Sweet Root Natural Area.

Sweet Root Natural Area. Furthermore, the natural area protects not only the plant and animal communities but also, as expanded in 1979, the amphibians and reptiles that live there, including both timber rattle-snakes and northern copperheads. In addition, crevices high in the cliffs provide a safe refuge for the threatened Allegheny woodrats. Other scarce mammal species found in the Sweet Root Natural Area are bobcats and red bats.

Unfortunately, we saw none of those creatures the day we parked our car at the Sweet Root Picnic Area and followed the white-blazed trail into the Sweet Root Gap itself. But American goldfinches called at the picnic area, and as we walked through a grove of second-growth oak and white pine, deer scattered off and gray squirrels ran ahead of us. Pileated and red-bellied woodpeckers, along with white-breasted nuthatches, worked over the trees, while the woods reverberated with the piping calls of spring peepers.

Beds of pink lady's slippers—wild orchids identifiable in summer only by their paired, green leaves—grow on either side of the trail, along with Indian pipe, Christmas fern, and New York fern. Loveliest of all are the distinctive white-veined, dark-green, ovate-shaped leaves of downy rattlesnake-plantain, a less flamboyant member of the Orchid family. According to Charles Darwin, English naturalist and evolutionist, the rattle-snake-plantain's genus—*Goodyera*—illustrates "the state of organs in a group of orchids now mostly extinct but the parents of living descendants." Admittedly, its evergreen leaves are more striking than the small greenish-white flowers that bloom in late summer crowded together on a single spike. But why the name "rattlesnake"? Some Native Americans, the story goes, believed the leaves to be an infallible cure for snakebite. But other Native Americans say the plant is named "rattlesnake" because its patterned leaves look like the pattern on a rattlesnake's belly. Although one modern herbalist claims that the leaves and rootstock of rattlesnake-plantain can be applied as a poultice to sores, skin rashes, bruises, and insect bites, he does not even mention snakebites. So, as is often the case with the common name of a plant, its true origin is uncertain.

You will hear Sweet Root Run long before you see it. After ascending a grassy hill, where the trail divides, take the right fork, following the sound of running water. Just before entering the gap, look for the Revolutionary War saltpeter cave across the run at the base of the cliffs. Continue along the barely discernible trail on the left bank of Sweet Root Run until you reach the heart of the 900-foot gap cut through Tussey Mountain. Most of the forest consists of hemlock, white pine, and yellow birch, but there is also a scattering of large oak, basswood, and tulip trees. So dense is the canopy that sunlight filters through only where there are gaps caused by fallen trees.

The temperature drops at least 10 degrees as you enter that virgin tract—natural air-conditioning that is welcome on a muggy summer day. Its coolness is reminiscent of the poet William Wordsworth's lines "It was a cove, a huge recess that keeps till June, December's snow." A cove, according to the *Oxford English Dictionary*, is "a recess with precipitous sides in the steep flank of a mountain," a phenomenon common in the English Lake District, Wordsworth's home territory. But it is also common in some parts of the United States, the *OED* says, where a cove is often called a "gap or pass." The *Century Dictionary and Cyclopedia* adds that the term "cove" is popular "in parts of the Appalachian range especially the Blue Ridge in Virginia where the coves are oval, almost entirely enclosed valleys"—which describes Sweet Root Gap.

In fact, Sweet Root Gap is a gap within what is called Beans Cove, but it is a gap that is so clogged with moss-covered boulders and fallen trees that passage is extremely difficult, except for water. Because it is a state forest natural area, fallen trees are left to rot and return all their nutrients to the soil. And since much of the old-growth timber in the gap has been blown down in the last several years, the way is quickly blocked.

For this reason, Sweet Root Natural Area is not a place for hikers, so visitors should spend their time enjoying the beauty of the setting, listening to the caroling of Carolina wrens and the raucous cries of blue jays, and watching the slow progress of orange-and-black giant millipedes crawling along the fallen trees. Those trees are productive nurseries for hemlock seedlings—a reminder that without human intervention young trees will someday become giants like their predecessors. Along with trees that are miniatures of the giants around them, the forest floor contains several pockets of jack-in-the-pulpits amid beds of fern and a blanket of moss.

It is easy to sit for a long time, lost in a vision of what primeval Pennsylvania had once looked like. And when you finally pull yourself together and climb back out into the human-altered world of smaller trees, you will be struck by the glaring summer sunshine.

From the intersection of U.S. 220 and U.S. 30 near Bedford: Follow Route 30 east 2.2 miles to Pa. 326. Follow 326 south 14.2 miles to the Sweet Root Natural Area. Note the following distances: 0.8 mile from U.S. 30 to a sharp right turn; 8.3 miles farther to the center of Rainsburg; 1.8 miles farther to the intersection on the right of the Blankley Road, top of Tussey Mountain; 3.3 miles to the Sweet Root Picnic Area; turn right 0.1 mile on the gravel road to the entrance to the access path into the natural area.

From Altoona: Follow U.S. 220 south to Bedford; from Johnstown follow Pa. 56 south to 220 just north of Bedford; from Exit 11 off the Pennsylvania Turnpike, follow commercial Route 220 north 0.2 mile, turn onto new Route 220, and follow it south 2 miles to the intersection with Route 30.

33   SIDELING HILL CREEK NATURAL AREA

Late spring is the ideal time to visit one of Pennsylvania's deserts: the Sideling Hill Creek shale barrens. Located in the extreme southwestern corner of Fulton County, the barrens is one of approximately 200 hot, dry shale outcroppings that extend from Huntingdon County in south-central Pennsylvania through the panhandle of western Maryland and down to southwestern Virginia and adjacent West Virginia.

The Sideling Hill Creek barrens is part of the larger 136-acre Sideling Hill Creek Natural Area purchased by the Western Pennsylvania Conservancy to preserve one of the most pristine and ecologically significant areas in central Appalachia. Rising out of mountain slopes in southeastern Bedford County, Sideling Hill Creek meanders 10 miles through narrow farm valleys in both Bedford and Fulton counties before crossing into western Maryland and ultimately flowing into the Potomac River.

Shale barrens consist of hard Devonian shale that breaks off to form talus and occur chiefly on the hot, south-facing slopes of hills. Surface temperatures on those barrens can reach as high as 150 degrees Fahrenheit, burning off most seeds that try to sprout on them. To survive under such conditions, plants need to have extensive root systems and be able to take the heat, rigorous requirements that eliminate most plants. Those that have colonized shale barrens are either endemics (plants found only on the barrens) such as cat's paw ragwort, or heat-loving plants—for in-

Shale barrens. Sideling Hill Creek Natural Area.

stance, Allegheny stonecrop and Virginia spiderwort. Those plants and many others grow on the Sideling Hill Creek shale barrens.

But one of the easiest plants to see—and a major reason for visiting the area—is the rare wetland wildflower golden club, which thrives in the pristine water of Sideling Hill Creek. A member of the Arum family, along with sweet flag, skunk cabbage, and jack-in-the-pulpit, golden club (*Orontium aquaticum*) has minute yellow flowers arranged on a golden, clublike spadix, an extension of its nearly foot-long stem, which is whitened on its upper end. Golden club is also known as "never wet" because its flat leaves have a waxy coating that sheds water.

In late May and early June, golden club, classified as rare in Pennsylvania, blossoms in Sideling Hill Creek just to the right of the ford. Two other creek plants, the state-endangered Tennessee pondweed (*Potamogeton tennessesnis*), which grows in the shallow, quiet pools along the stream, and the rare riverweed, also thrive in the creek's pristine waters. In addition, there are two rare mussels, a rare fish (the Potomac sculpin), and an unusual freshwater sponge (*Spongilla lacustros*), of interest to aquatic biologists. On the barren itself, there are four species of rare moths, including the Packard's lichen moth (*Cisthene packardii*), and five rare plants.

To get a view of the Sideling Hill Creek barrens, stand at the ford and look downstream (left), and you will see a large part of the central portion of the barrens studded with stunted trees and shrubs. This barrens extends both upstream and downstream and covers nearly 50 acres, but most of the area is steep and difficult to climb. Better for you and the plants to don a pair of rubber boots and wade downstream along the water's edge to where the steep cliffs reach the stream. By poking slowly along, eyes and ears alert, you will see an abundance of interesting plants and birds in a beautiful, canyon-like setting.

The first red-shale outcropping has a large display of Allegheny stonecrop (*Sedum telephioides*). Also known as wild live-forever and American orpine, it is a close relative of a favorite garden plant, the European stonecrop. Its attractive pale, reddish-tinged, gray-green leaves are succulent and oval-shaped, and in August and September the plant sports flat-topped clusters of white-to-dark-pink flowers.

Before reaching that outcropping, you need to ease yourself over and around uprooted trees along the bank. From there, during our visit, a pair of Louisiana waterthrushes flew up in great excitement, a signal that they had a nest somewhere in the stream bank. Usually they choose the south side of a stream in which to dig a shallow cup in the bank's dirt, fill the cup with fallen leaves, and line it with grasses, small rootlets, plant stems, and moss sporophytes. Their four to six young are hatched by the end of May and fledge ten days later, but the parents continue protecting them for many more weeks.

Other bird species you might hear or see include eastern wood pewees, northern cardinals, eastern phoebes (which like to plaster their nests underneath the rocky ledges), indigo buntings, gray catbirds, red-eyed vireos, scarlet tanagers, blue-gray gnatcatchers, field sparrows, and rufous-sided towhees. Cedar waxwings (perhaps attracted by the eastern red cedar that grows on the barrens), yellow-billed cuckoos, and northern orioles are also present as part of the fine mixture of both woodland and field bird species that live in the area. Turkey vultures often circle overhead, and red-tailed hawks float past above the creek.

Continue picking your way along the edge of the barrens in search of such rock-loving wildflowers as hairy beardtongue, Virginia spiderwort, columbine, and alumroot, as well as the fern ebony spleenwort and several species of lichens and mosses. While the dark-blue, three-petaled spiderwort has almost finished blooming by early June, the handsome alumroot is at its height. A member of the Saxifrage family, it has greenish, bell-shaped flowers drooping from short branching stems arranged alternately along a single stem. A cluster of maple-shaped leaves grows farther down the stem and around its base. Its root is strongly astringent and produces an alum-like effect when applied to the tongue, hence its common name.

In addition to the Allegheny stonecrop, other rare-to-Pennsylvania barrens plants include dwarf spirea (also known as corymbed spirea or birch-leaved meadowsweet), Harris's or leather-leaved goldenrod (the earliest and longest-blooming of the goldenrods, which often opens in May), and the small-flowered crowfoot.

But the best endemic, in this section of the barrens, is the Pennsylvania-endangered cat's paw ragwort (*Senecio antennariifolius*), which has adaptations common to many plants that grow in hot, dry areas—namely, upper leaf surfaces that are whitened to reflect the heat, a covering of dense hairs on the lower leaf surfaces to insulate the plant, and a crowded rosette of leaves growing close to the ground to protect the plant from the drying wind and intense heat reflected from the shale. Because the cat's paw ragwort grows in an isolated, steep area it is better left alone.

The rarest plant associated with Sideling Hill Creek, harperella, is a globally rare plant and has been found only on gravel shoals and in rock crevices on the Maryland portion of the creek. Like the other rare Pennsylvania plants, it is protected.

On the rocky stream bank you will also find a host of other more common wildflowers, such as the yellow-flowered stargrass, wild garlic, and the attractive violet wood-sorrel with its cloverlike leaves and rose-purple or purplish-violet flaring, five-petaled blossoms. Altogether a June day at the Sideling Hill Creek Natural Area will reward the diligent plant-lover with many surprises over a small portion of ground. Also, be on the lookout for snakes and lizards on the shale outcroppings, and for frogs at the creek's edge.

During your visit to this remote spot you will probably encounter no one else. Be sure to stay on the left side of the creek, which is the only portion owned by the Western Pennsylvania Conservancy. If you're lucky, the day will be relatively cool and perfumed by the abundance of multiflora roses that grow in the area. Tiger swallowtails will flutter past, a pickerel frog will leap at your feet, and you will wonder why shale barrens are referred to as Pennsylvania's deserts.

Eastbound, from Exit 11, Bedford, of the Pennsylvania Turnpike: Follow Business Route U.S. 220 north about 200 yards and enter new Route 220. Follow 220 south about 2 miles, then follow U.S. Route 30 east about 8 miles and take the exit off Route 30 into the center of Everett. At the second traffic light in Everett, turn right onto Pa. 26 south.

Westbound, from the turnpike Exit 12, Breezewood: Follow U.S. 30 west about 8 miles and take Business Route 30 into the center of Everett. Turn left at the first traffic light on Pa. 26 south. From Everett, follow Pa. 26 south. After 7.5 miles, Route 26 turns to the right in the village of Clearville. Follow 26 another 13.1 miles, over a very winding, scenic route, to a stop sign where Route 26 turns right. (Alternate: Continue straight ahead in the center of Clearville, turn right at a Y-intersection 0.6 mile from Clearville, and follow a well-paved road that is less windy and equally as scenic as Route 26 for 12.3 miles to the same intersection.) From the stop sign 13.1 miles south of Clearville, turn right and follow Pa. 26 another 2.7 miles to the intersection with Pa. 484. Turn left and follow 484 east 0.9 mile and turn right onto an unmarked gravel road. The road goes up a small hill and down to a ford through Sideling Hill Creek, 0.4 mile from the pavement. Park on the side of the road without blocking a lane near the ford.

WESTERN PENNSYLVANIA

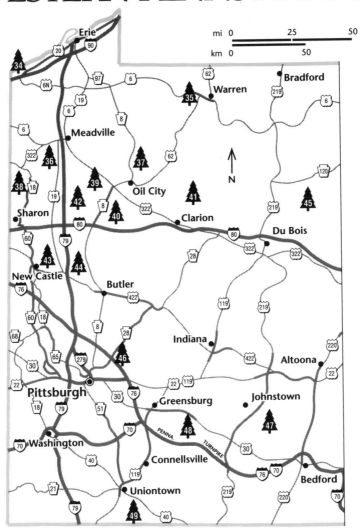

34. DAVID M. RODERICK WILDLIFE RESERVE
35. ANDERS RUN NATURAL AREA
36. CONNEAUT MARSH
37. OIL CREEK STATE PARK
38. BRUCKER GREAT BLUE HERON SANCTUARY OF THIEL COLLEGE
39. FRENCH CREEK
40. CLEAR CREEK STATE FOREST / ALLEGHENY RIVER AREA
41. CLARION RIVER
42. PINE SWAMP NATURAL AREA

43. FRINGED GENTIAN FEN NATURAL AREA
44. MORAINE STATE PARK AND MILLER ESKER NATURAL AREA
45. ELK-WATCHING
46. RACHEL CARSON HOMESTEAD AND TRAIL
47. BOG PATH AND BOULDER TRAIL
48. POWDERMILL NATURE RESERVE AND LINN RUN STATE PARK
49. QUEBEC RUN WILD AREA

34 DAVID M. RODERICK WILDLIFE RESERVE

On a windy summer day, visitors can stand on steep bluffs at the David M. Roderick Wildlife Reserve and watch the waves of Lake Erie crash against the rock beach. Water, sand, woods, and wildlife are all there is to see. It is as if they have been transported to one of the world's last wild shores.

Officially dedicated in July 1991, this 3,131-acre reserve on the south shore of Lake Erie is part of a 5,000-acre tract that spans the Pennsylvania-Ohio border. It used to be owned by United States Steel Corporation (now USX), having been purchased by Andrew Carnegie in 1900–1901 as a site for a major steel mill, but after resurfacing in the 1960s, plans for the steel mill were finally abandoned. Then, under David M. Roderick, chief executive officer of USX at the time, the property was purchased by the Richard King Mellon Foundation. The Mellon Foundation conveyed it to the Western Pennsylvania Conservancy, which in turn sold it to the Pennsylvania Game Commission.

In the long interim between the shelving of the Carnegie steel mill plant and the 1960s revival, U.S. Steel attempted to utilize the land in a variety of ways. First, the wooded areas were subdivided into 290 farm parcels, which were leased to farmers and called Conneaut Farms. Because 60 percent of the tract is a wetland, however, none of the farms thrived. Next, 12 natural-gas wells were drilled there in the 1940s, but eventually abandoned. The company also leased the lakefront property to people for cottages. However, the bluffs on which they built the structures eroded rapidly because of Lake Erie's high water levels. Still trying to make a profit from the uncooperative land, the company sold the timber rights for trees eight inches or more in diameter.

After the logging ended in 1960, the land lay fallow, slowly reverting to almost impenetrable thickets and young woodlands interspersed throughout with small wetlands. Today, the reserve provides a haven for a wide variety of wildlife, such as fox squirrels, white-tailed deer, and cottontail rabbits.

Lake Erie shoreline. David M. Roderick Wildlife Reserve.

Primarily, though, it is a place for the birds. Waterfowl, gamebirds, and songbirds thrive on different portions of the property. To see the greatest number of species, the spring and fall migration periods are best. Many spring-migrating birds use the reserve to fuel up before flying across Lake Erie, so on a good day in April bird-watchers can easily tally 100 species.

Earlier, in March, American woodcocks engage in their annual courtship rituals from dusk to dark. Back in 1987, even before the Game Commission acquired the land, a Game Commission biologist determined that the tract was one of the state's best woodcock breeding grounds. To keep it that way, the Game Commission used a Royer upland vegetation cutter to eliminate the shrubs and saplings that had filled-in the open areas woodcocks need for their courtship displays. They used the same machine to create wildlife feeding strips in thickets, to open old, overgrown roads, and to make parking areas.

To attract wood ducks and other waterfowl, the Game Commission released a pair of beaver in the forested wetlands. The trees they felled provided good cover along the water's edge. The hope is that such management efforts will attract breeding rails, bitterns, and black terns, in addition to waterfowl.

On a March day when the wind is from the southwest, raptor-watching is also productive. Bald eagles, ospreys, merlins, and northern goshawks are possible sightings, along with the more common hawk species. At least two rare state songbirds have been sighted in November, the second-ever state record for a Bohemian waxwing in 1992 and for a warbling vireo in 1993.

But summer is the best time to see breeding birds. During Pennsylvania's breeding-bird atlasing period—a statewide survey conducted from 1983 through 1989 by more than 2,000 volunteer birders—59 species were verified. Most interesting is the large colony of bank swallows that excavate nest sites one to four feet deep in the fine clays and silts that compose the shoreline bluffs. Such Wisconsin glacial deposits are prime nesting spots for Pennsylvania's smallest swallow species.

The Game Commission is committed to building a good trail system on the property. The most accessible one is reached by following Lake Road west from the monument parking lot 0.1 mile until it intersects with State Line Road. Turn left and go 0.5 mile to the trail entrance on the left. This trail follows the path of an abandoned railroad line that intersects the center of the reserve. On a mid-June walk along this trail, we identified a nice mix of songbirds—rose-breasted grosbeak, great-crested flycatcher, veery, wood thrush, American redstart, yellow warbler, yellow-throated vireo, and alder, willow, and least flycatchers. It is also possible to glimpse common snipes and American woodcocks in the wetlands.

This trail continues for 1.4 miles until it intersects with Rudd Road. You can walk only a portion of it and then retrace your steps, or walk an easy, level 4.4-mile circuit by walking left on Rudd Road toward the lake and left again on Lake Road back toward your car.

On a calm, warm day when the water is still, it is possible to descend to the beach below the confluence of Rudd Road and Lake Road and follow it west, with some shallow wading where the water meets the cliffs, for 2.1 miles to Turkey Creek, 0.6 mile beyond the Ohio line. Then turn left until you reach a small, unused concrete bridge. Turn left again and follow an abandoned road back to State Line and Lake Shore roads. Continue east on Lake Shore Road until you reach Rudd Road. This is approximately a four-mile circuit, but it gives hikers an excellent view of the bank swallow nesting area. It is also the longest remaining stretch of undeveloped lakefront on the south shore of Lake Erie between Buffalo, New York, and Toledo, Ohio.

As David Roderick commented during the dedication ceremonies, the land was not "destined to be the site of a mill—either in 1900 or 1980. . . ."

Its destiny [was to be] set aside as an area to be maintained in its natural state for the benefit of the public."

From the Erie area: Follow Interstate 79 south to Interstate 90, then take 90 west nearly 19 miles to Exit 1. Drive north on U.S. 6 north 0.5 mile to the intersection with U.S. 20. Turn left and follow Route 20 west 1.4 miles to the intersection with Pa. Route 5. About 100 yards farther west on Route 20, turn right on Rudd Road and follow it north toward Lake Erie. After 2.5 miles, turn left at a T-intersection and follow Lake Road 1.3 miles to the parking area for the Roderick Reserve Monument.

35   ANDERS RUN NATURAL AREA

Most of western Pennsylvania was cut over in the latter part of the nineteenth century, but the 96-acre Anders Run Natural Area, six miles west of Warren, was logged sometime during the first two decades of the 1800s—for the first and last time. Today this second-growth forest has white pine and hemlock trees 170 years old, many standing 120 feet high with trunk diameters of more than 40 inches. Not an ancient forest by northwestern American standards, and not a climax (stable and self-perpetuating) forest by northeastern American standards, it nevertheless represents, according to the Western Pennsylvania Conservancy, which originally purchased the land in late 1987, "the best young stand of this forest type in western Pennsylvania."

If the trees of Anders Run Natural Area had never been cut, the white pines, which tolerate sunny openings, would be dead or dying, being replaced inexorably by shade-loving climax species of hemlock and northern hardwoods. This process is now occurring in the virgin timber stands at Hearts Content Natural Area and Cook Forest State Park. Left alone over the next several centuries, the Anders Run Natural Area will serve for future generations as a remnant window to what much of Pennsylvania once looked like.

Second-growth forest. Anders Run Natural Area.

The land was turned over to the Pennsylvania Bureau of Forestry in 1989 and is now the Anders Run Natural Area within the Cornplanter State Forest. The Bureau has expanded the trail system to 1.8 miles, built two wooden bridges and several wooden benches, and erected numerous trail signs.

From the parking lot, walk down toward the stream valley through a mostly oak woods with a line of tall white pines to the left of the trail. If you visit in early autumn, acorns may fall with almost the same frequency as raindrops, and those woods will chatter with chipmunks. After a fifth of a mile you will reach the same paved road that had looped around the oak woods. Turn left and follow that road another fifth of a mile until you see a yellow-blazed trail leading off to the right. Follow it down into the heart of the stream valley.

You may be greeted by the scolding calls of red squirrels. Although the noise from the squirrels will quickly subside, the steady parade of vehicles on the paved road will serve as a constant reminder that this patch of primeval woods is not in a primeval place. But here in the East such fragmented remnants are all we have left even of excellent second-growth forest.

In this case, the saving of Anders Run Natural Area began back in 1963 when the National Forge Company planned a timber sale on their land, which included Anders Run and surrounding woodlands. The Northern Allegheny Conservation Association suggested that they exclude the white pine forest from their timbering plans, and the company agreed.

In 1987 National Forge generously sold the property for half its fair market value. The final price was paid by the Western Pennsylvania Conservancy, the Northern Allegheny Conservation Association, and the De-Frees Family Foundation—the latter two, like National Forge, based in Warren. Local pride, in fact, is not only what saved the tract originally but also what has fueled the improvements to the site, bankrolled by the Pennsylvania Bureau of Forestry.

Following the trail through the stream valley, look for the leaves of a bevy of spring wildflowers—hepatica, Solomon's seal, wild geranium, painted trillium, wild ginger, white Clintonia, Indian cucumber-root, bunchberry, several violet species, foamflower, and pink lady's slipper—while the blackened, dried remains of Indian pipes testify to their ghostly presence in summer. But during early autumn, a large bed of parasitic beechdrops grows beneath an enormous beech tree. Along the trail there is also a scattering of woodland aster and goldenrod species. Most colorful of all are the deep-blue berries of blue cohosh, and the white berries, each with a single red dot, of white baneberry or "doll's eyes."

The usual damp woods ferns—New York, sensitive, cinnamon, Christmas, and several woodland fern species—grow along the stream, but once you reach the first wooden bridge and cross it you will be in a maidenhair fern zone, which continues as you climb the hillside. Near the top of the trail, notice the "No trespassing" sign ahead, erected by Allegheny Forestry Incorporated—proud members, so the sign declares, of the Pennsylvania Landowners Association.

The contrast between the privately and publicly owned land is startling. The former is "twig timber," smaller even than the usual pole timber, while just over the line on public land grows a white pine that is more than 45 inches in diameter. The trail parallels the property line for several hundred feet, so you can alternately look down at the healthy, natural interior of Anders Run and then over at the impenetrable brush of the private land—from the Pennsylvania of centuries ago to the Pennsylvania of today.

What creatures and plants disappeared as Pennsylvania's old-growth (climax) forests were leveled in the last century? How much biodiversity continues to be lost with subsequent cuttings? No one knows, but scientists suspect that with each cutting the land's ability to regenerate is reduced and numbers, if not species, decline. Chris Maser, author of a poignant elegy to northwestern old-growth forests, *Forest Primeval: The Natural History of an Ancient Forest,* is an advocate of what he calls "restoration forestry," in which we do not take more from the land than we return. He writes: "The key to and the value of restoration is in the thought process it implies. And part of this process is saving as much of Nature's ancient forest as humanly possible so that we and future generations can learn how to restore and sustain the forests of the world for all of humanity."

Unfortunately Pennsylvania does not have the millions of contiguous acres of ancient forest that still exist in the northwestern United States. Instead, the commonwealth has 25,000 acres of ancient forest in small, scattered tracts. Still, the existence of a place like Anders Run Natural Area should help Pennsylvania's "restoration forestry" projects as well, something visitors should think about as they descend the steep trail, cross a second bridge over Anders Run and a gravel road, and finally plunge back into the second-growth forest on the last lap of their walk. This drier section, which parallels the gravel road, has a scattering of white pine among the oak and features enormous fern-covered boulders with large trees perched on top, their exposed roots splaying down over the rocks to reach the forest floor. It was there we surprised a buck close-up and listened to a singing red-eyed vireo. Finally you will emerge above the parking lot and cross the paved road, having come full circle.

The Pennsylvania Bureau of Forestry's Warren office says that the red oak trees on the property are of exceptional quality. Consequently, they collect the acorns from some of the best trees for the state nursery, so they can improve the red oak strain they are currently growing. The growth rate of the other species at Anders Run is incredibly fast by forestry standards, and foresters attribute that to the unusually rich soil. Could it be that the soil has had such a long time to regenerate? Isn't this, in fact, an excellent example of "restoration forestry"?

Whatever the answer, the trees of Anders Run will continue to be allowed to reach their full maturity, then molder and die at their own rate, providing both spiritual nourishment and seed trees for perpetuity.

For further information contact: Pennsylvania Bureau of Forestry, 323 North State Street, Warren, PA 16365, or call 814-723-6951 for a trail brochure.

From Warren: Follow U.S. 6 west 5.7 miles and then bear right off the freeway for U.S. 62 south. After proceeding 0.5 mile, turn right before the bridge over the

Allegheny River where the sign indicates Buckaloons Recreation Area. Go 0.7 mile and turn left on Dunns Eddy River Road. Drive 1 mile and pull into the parking area for Cornplanter State Forest, Anders Run Natural Area, on the left.

36   CONNEAUT MARSH

The water came within inches of the road, the day we launched our canoe into Conneaut Marsh. It had been raining for weeks, filling the marsh to capacity, but on this May morning the sun shone and a stiff breeze riffled the water. We were eager to see what Conneaut Marsh in southern Crawford County had to offer in the way of wildlife. Known locally as Geneva Marsh, this 5,499-acre wetland, which stretches 13 miles between Conneaut Lake and French Creek, is also State Game Lands 213.

"Conneaut" is the English spelling of the Iroquoian "Konn Knu Yaut," which means "Melted Snow Water Lake." As part of the glaciated Allegheny Plateau in northwestern Pennsylvania, the long, flat-bottomed valley containing the marsh had been filled with glacial outwash during the Illinoian and Wisconsin ice ages 17,000 years ago. Conneaut Lake itself, Pennsylvania's largest natural inland lake, is classified by geologists as a "kettle lake" because it was formed in a deep depression left when a huge ice block surrounded by sediment melted.

Today Conneaut Lake covers 938 acres and is the major source of the marsh's water. The marsh is 1,060 feet above sea level and encircled by rolling uplands 1,300 to 1,400 feet in height.

To the uninitiated, Conneaut Marsh can be a confusing maze, but there is a navigable channel for canoeists. It runs from Geneva Dike near the town of Geneva to the Mud Pike bridge turnaround, a route through the open pond and into the wooded swamp that is easy to negotiate during high water.

To help the Pennsylvania Game Commission acquire key parcels of the area, in 1976 the Western Pennsylvania Conservancy purchased 684 acres of the marsh's western edge, which includes the outflow of Conneaut Marsh. They acquired the second piece, 175 acres on the marsh's eastern

Wooded swamp near Mud Pike bridge. Conneaut Marsh.

edge, in 1981. That portion contains the only section of Conneaut Outlet that has not been channelized or dredged. Both portions were then turned over to the Game Commission.

Conneaut Marsh, like so many of our nation's once bountiful numbers of wetlands, was tampered with, back in 1868 when the Pennsylvania legislature passed an act providing for draining the marsh. A stream-dredging machine was purchased, and a channel 8 feet deep and 16 feet wide was dredged from the lake to within two and a half miles of French Creek. Then the marsh was drained and cattle were grazed up to the edges of the channel.

According to local residents, the marsh remained a meadow until the 1920s, when humans once again interfered by building a causeway across the marsh for Route 19. But other land-use changes also helped the meadow revert to the marsh it had once been. The channel filled in over the years with soil washed in from surrounding farmlands. Ditches dug in the fields, as well as along the new roads and highways, caused rainfall once held in the soil to flow directly into streams and marshes.

This reversion to the natural state must have pleased a wide range of outdoor people—waterfowl hunters who still have spectacular shooting October through December during migration, fishers who know the marsh as a good place for northern pike and largemouth bass, and wildlife-watchers who have seen bobcats, muskrats, beaver, opossums, and raccoons, in addition to such marsh birds as wood ducks, marsh wrens, black terns, and Virginia, king, and sora rails, as well as nesting bald eagles.

However, paddling a canoe and holding binoculars steady at the same time is nearly impossible, so most bird-identification is done by ear. After putting your canoe in at Geneva Dike, paddle northwest along the channel through the open marsh. You will rarely be out of earshot of gabbling Canada geese, and you might even spot a goose sitting on a nest. Red-tailed hawks float overhead; great blue herons and green-backed herons take off as you approach them. Marshy islands throughout the pond area are dotted with muskrat lodges, and the water itself roils with spawning carp, many of them more than two feet long.

But the essence of a marsh is the continual "okalee" songs of red-winged blackbirds. Along with eastern kingbirds, they are the most visible and vocal birds in the open marsh.

Once you pilot your way around the beaver dam in the stream and enter the wooded swamp, the bird population gradually changes from meadow birds—common yellowthroats, yellow warblers, bluebirds, and song sparrows—to birds common in wooded areas: eastern wood pe-wees, great-crested flycatchers, and scarlet tanagers. Best of all are the singing prothonotary warblers, "golden birds of wooded swamps," as ornithologist-artist Roger Tory Peterson calls those birds with deep-yellow heads and breasts and bluish-gray wings and tails.

This section of the outlet is more like a slow-moving woodland creek. Proceed half a mile until you reach the turnaround at the Mud Pike bridge. Then retrace your route back to the Geneva Dike.

Throughout the marsh, you will often be accompanied by unseen reptiles and amphibians—turtles that sink out of sight before you can identify them, bullfrogs whose muted courtship roaring reverberates from marshy vegetation, spring peepers emitting their high-pitched "songs of spring." But the silent northern water snakes are not shy. Frequently snake heads emerge from the water and swim beside a canoe, and every overhanging limb seems to hold a snake basking in the sunshine.

As with every wild creature you see, watch but do not interfere. Each has its reason for being; each fits into that niche we label "marsh."

From Pittsburgh: Follow Interstate 79 north approximately 70 miles to Exit 35. Drive west on Pa. 285 for 2.7 miles and turn right in the village of Geneva. Drive

1.1 miles to a Y in the road, and park in the wide area off the road at the Geneva Dike.

37   OIL CREEK STATE PARK

"Oil Creek, which has become celebrated as the site of the richest oil-producing region on earth at the present day, is a tortuous mountain stream, taking its rise in the northern part of the state of Pennsylvania . . . and after a course of about thirty miles . . . [emptying] into the Allegheny River seven miles above the town of Franklin. The valley through which Oil Creek takes its course is narrow, and flanked on each side by high and rugged hills, on the top of which are broad fields of excellent farming land. The scenery on Oil Creek at one time, no doubt, was quite picturesque, but now the bottomlands are dotted with tall derricks, wooden engine-houses, and iron smokestacks, out of which columns of black smoke roll upward to the clouds. The pines and hemlocks are cleared from the mountainsides, and all is busy life."

So wrote an anonymous author in *Harper's New Monthly Magazine* in April 1865, less than six years after the discovery of oil near Oil Creek. The local *Venango Spectator* put it more bluntly 12 years later: "This Oil Creek used to be one of the purest streams in the United States and now what is it like? Why it is the most filthy stream on God's footstool, and you cannot find a fish in it from Oil City to Titusville."

Today, bass and trout are abundant in Oil Creek. Hemlocks and deciduous trees cover the steep slopes on either side of the creek, and once again the scenery is "picturesque." In Oil Creek State Park itself, little remains of the oil-boom days but abandoned buildings and rusting oil pumps overgrown with vegetation. Petroleum Centre, once described as "a metropolis of rum and debauchery," consists mostly of plaques for a self-guided walking tour of the oil boom town just outside the park office. An excellent little museum provides visitors with a feel for how it was then, as well as how it has reverted back to the original scenic beauty before "Colonel" Edwin Drake struck oil on August 27, 1859.

Flowering dogwood in bloom along the Oil Creek Hiking Trail. Oil Creek
State Park.

Oil Creek State Park has a whole stack of attractions for visitors, including a 9.7-mile paved biking trail that brings between 30,000 and 40,000 visitors a year. On the lovely day in May when we visited, bicyclists of all ages whizzed by, obviously having a wonderful time.

But we found our own place in the park along the extensive hiking-trail system, choosing a moderately strenuous, seven-mile loop that grants visitors peace, serenity, beauty, and solitude. You will probably not pass a single hiker the entire length of the trail, even though the bike trail is crowded, the picnic areas are full, and Petroleum Centre is pulsing with humanity interested in history, recreation, and fishing.

Yet the moment you enter the white-blazed trail behind the park office, human-made noise begins to fade. Within minutes, birdsong replaces it: the drawn out "pee-a-wees" of eastern wood pewees, the "buzzing" of blue-gray gnatcatchers, the unending song of red-eyed vireos, the "che-becs" of least flycatchers, the "teacher, teacher, teacher" of ovenbirds, the "drink-your-tea" of rufous-sided towhees. Chipmunks skitter over dried leaves, and once we heard a thrashing through the forest that sounded more like a black bear than a white-tailed deer.

After 0.2 mile, the white-blazed trail joins the main yellow-blazed trail, part of the 36-mile Oil Creek Hiking Trail loop, which runs along both the east and the west side of Oil Creek from Drake Well in the north to Petroleum Centre in the south.

In this moderately uphill portion of the trail, moss-covered boulders support several birch saplings, red elderberry shrubs, and common poly-pody ferns. The woods floor in spring is a wild garden of Solomon's seal, jack-in-the-pulpit, skunk cabbage, golden ragwort, Canada mayflower, wild sarsaparilla, and perfoliate bellwort.

Once the trail levels off, it follows northeast along the ridgetop with hemlock spilling down the steep slope to the left and a deciduous forest spreading off to the right. In the wet areas along the trail, beautiful stands of interrupted, sensitive, Christmas, and cinnamon ferns thrive. Mayapples, Indian cucumber-root, wild geranium, and several species of white, lilac, and yellow violets also like the moisture. So do the American toads, which sometimes sing along with American redstarts, black-and-white warblers, and black-throated blue warblers on early May days.

Under the largest hemlock is the only wooden bench along this section of the trail, a good place to pause and rest before crossing the tornado-damaged area of uprooted large trees and descending the hill to a dirt road.

Then you enter the woods again, this time following Hemlock Run upstream through a forest of hemlock, birch, and white oak growing amid an understory of Christmas and spinulose wood ferns, wood anemone, yellow mandarin, Canada mayflower, and red trillium or "wake robin." Best of all, though, is the chance to see a singing "fiery-throat"— the brilliant, orange-throated Blackburnian warbler.

At a trail intersection marked with a sign saying "Bridge at Pioneer .7, West Side Trail 2.3," turn left onto the white-blazed trail and walk through an "alley" of young hemlocks downhill to the floodplain of Hemlock Run. Here, on flat rocks, is an ideal place to pause and eat a trail lunch, because it is almost the halfway point along the seven-mile trail. Besides, you need rest and fortification for the steep ascent up the other side of the stream— a 25- to 45-degree slope for nearly a quarter-mile.

The trail then drops abruptly down to the bike path. If you have had enough by then, turn left and follow the bike trail back to Petroleum Centre. Otherwise, the steepest part of the trail now behind you, turn right over the biking bridge, and 50 feet beyond pick up the white-blazed trail on the left.

Again the trail ascends, but this time gently and paralleling Pioneer Run. Look for blooming foamflower and the leaves of April-bloomers— trailing arbutus, trout-lily, skunk cabbage, and cut-leaved toothwort. Your rewards for persisting along this section of the trail are a view of Greg Falls and then, after crossing Pioneer Run on a log, an entire hillside of blooming white trillium interspersed with maidenhair fern and foamflower.

Then make your final ascent, following the trail high above Pioneer Run, crossing a powerline right-of-way and a scenic overlook of Oil Creek and the bike trail far below, and passing several dilapidated buildings to the left of the trail. Once you reach a paved road, you can either follow it left back to the park office, or cross it and add another half-mile on to your walk by taking a trail through old fields and young growth alive with the brilliance of rose-breasted grosbeaks, yellow warblers, and possibly even a migrating Canada warbler wearing its necklace of black over a bright-yellow neck and breast.

When you reach a wide swath in the forest, turn left, follow it for less than half a mile, and emerge finally at the bridge crossing over to Petroleum Centre. You will have covered less than one-fifth of the length of the major hiking trail, but had you continued on the yellow-blazed trail above Hemlock Run, you would have reached the first of two Adirondack shelter areas for backpackers along the loop trail. Each area has six camping shelters with stone fireplaces, making it possible for long-distance hikers to complete the entire trail in two and a half days. Reservations are needed to use the shelters, so call 814-676-5915. The park office has maps and friendly personnel to answer your questions.

The possibilities at Oil Creek State Park for enjoying the outdoors include canoeing from March until June, hunting, picnicking, and cross-country skiing. Two car-camping facilities adjacent to the park are reasonably priced and offer a wide variety of recreational opportunities.

From Pittsburgh: Take Pa. 8 north to Oil City. As you enter Oil City, take the Route 8 bypass. From the traffic light at the end of the bypass, continue north on Pa. 8 another 3.3 miles to the second bridge over Oil Creek. Turn right onto a narrow road just beyond the bridge (sign to Oil Creek State Park). Follow the road 0.9 mile to an intersection; turn right and cross a one-lane bridge over the creek. The park administration office is 0.1 mile beyond the bridge on the left.

38   BRUCKER GREAT BLUE HERON SANCTUARY OF THIEL COLLEGE

If seeing great blue herons by the hundreds appeals to you, then the Brucker Great Blue Heron Sanctuary of Thiel College in Mercer County is *the* place to visit from late February until early May. There you can sit in a covered shelter, binoculars in hand, and watch the largest great blue heron rookery in Pennsylvania set up housekeeping for the year.

Don't expect water or a wilderness setting. Great blue herons, or at least the ones using the sanctuary, apparently lack an aesthetic sense. A four-lane highway is all that separates them from the thriving Greenville-Reynolds Development Corporation, a former World War II army replacement depot now filled with businesses producing everything from plastic sacks to specialty steel. Adjacent to the sanctuary itself is a truck-

Great blue herons and their nests. Brucker Great Blue Heron Sanctuary of Thiel College.

ing company. Highway traffic and a nearby railroad line provide background noise.

The herons don't mind crowding either. Although the sanctuary consists of 45 acres of woodland, they occupy only 10 acres, in which they have constructed 235 nests in 93 trees. Only the tallest oak, hickory, and ash trees are used as nesting trees, with each tree supporting between 5 and 10 nests. The champion nesting tree contains 17 nests!

Luckily for great blue heron aficionados, the favored 10 acres include the boundary trees along an open field that separates the viewing shelter from the colony. Some visitors who arrive shortly after dawn have even been able to watch the herons close-up, foraging on the field.

Great blue herons are sensitive to human disturbance during nesting time, so the land beneath the rookery is closed from February 1 until September 1. It was, in fact, their sensitivity to human disturbance that led to the founding of the sanctuary.

Edward Brucker, a retired businessman from nearby Masury, Ohio, had been observing the rookery since 1978, when the company he had been working for in Cleveland transferred him to their Sharon, Pennsylvania, facility. To Brucker, an avid fisherman, being near well-watered Mercer

County was an incentive not only to get out and fish but also to do some bird work.

"Bird work" has always meant studying great blue herons. Although Brucker is a serious amateur birder where great blue herons are concerned, he is not a bird-watcher. He prefers to concentrate all his research efforts on one species. Year after year he has sent in his data to the Colonial Bird Register, a program of Cornell University's Laboratory of Ornithology, and to the Pennsylvania Game Commission.

By 1985, Brucker knew a lot about great blue herons. He had watched the colony steadily increase its numbers, and he recognized its uniqueness as the largest landlocked great blue heron colony in Pennsylvania, and also one of the largest inland monospecific heronries in the northeastern United States.

Then, during a visit to the rookery in April 1985, Brucker encountered a lumbering operation hard at work less than 200 feet from the closest nests. They could not have picked a worse time to clear a swath of land so a gas company could replace an existing main distribution line carrying gas from Pennsylvania into Ohio.

Clearly disturbed by the noise, great blue herons began deserting their nests with eggs. Before Brucker persuaded the superintendent of the company to postpone tree-cutting and construction of the line for three weeks until the remaining herons had hatched their families, 17 of the then 95 nests were abandoned. But after the three-week hiatus, the herons did adapt to the resumption of lumbering once their eggs became nestlings.

Eleven months later, Brucker encountered the second and more serious threat to the rookery—loss of habitat. A Pennsylvania-based lumber company had bought timbering rights to the land from two landowners, and the company intended to cut down all the mature trees, including those containing nests. With the help and advice of a local sportsman, a biology professor from Thiel College, and the district game protector for the Pennsylvania Game Commission, Brucker contacted an agent for the U.S. Fish and Wildlife Service who was able to halt the operation until August 1, because the cutting of any nest tree was considered an attempt to kill the birds, a clear violation of the U.S. Migratory Bird Treaty Act. But once nesting was over for the year, logging could be resumed.

This gave Brucker and his associates four months to develop a plan to protect the rookery. First they formed a nonprofit corporation called "The Brucker Great Blue Heron Sanctuary," which had three stated objectives:

(1) to preserve the present great blue heron nesting area and develop additional conducive habitat area, (2) to promote and coordinate the conservation of the natural resources within the boundaries of land owned, leased, or otherwise developed by the corporation located in Mercer County, and (3) to conduct educational and scientific programs related to the resources within the boundaries of the sanctuary. By August 7, the sanctuary was a legal, perpetual nonprofit organization.

Concurrently they talked to the three major landowners of the area, one of which was Greenville-Reynolds. Brucker convinced them of the importance of saving the colony. "The herons," he told them, "could be a real plus for the community," by attracting businesses that were interested in quality of life for their employees. Every community trying to attract new businesses offers low taxes, adequate water, electricity, and a skilled labor force, but how many can offer an environment clean enough to support a great blue heron sanctuary? he argued. Furthermore, what does that say about a community's commitment to what he called the "total quality of life"?

Such reasoning, bolstered by concentrated local media coverage in 12 county newspapers and the support of the Mercer County Federation of Sportsmen, as well as the Bartramian Audubon Society, led to an agreement among the landowners to protect the site. The logging company generously donated the 12.5 acres where the heron nests were located.

That was only the beginning. Since then, although the number of herons ebbs and flows according to weather conditions, community interest and support continue to escalate. Local businesses have donated materials to build a visitor parking lot, membership in the sanctuary has increased, and Brucker and his speakers bureau have been presenting more and more programs to schoolchildren and local clubs about the great blue herons in general and the sanctuary in particular. Brucker also edits the fine newsletter that comes out twice a year, and of course continues to monitor the rookery.

In early 1993, some 22.5 acres of the 45-acre sanctuary were donated to Thiel College in nearby Greenville by the Bruckers and the Greenville-Reynolds Development Corporation. Because educating the public remains the major thrust of the sanctuary, Brucker hopes this will be an opportunity to improve the sanctuary's educational program, as well as provide the college and its students with a valuable resource for observation and research.

Great blue herons are the largest members of the heron family in the United States and Canada. They stand four feet tall, weigh between six and eight pounds, and have a seven-foot wingspan. Most of their nicknames—"big blue heron," "blue crane," and "common blue crane"—refer to their bluish-gray bodies. Their less complimentary name—"shitepoke"—is an allusion to their habit of moving their bowels immediately after they eat.

Except during breeding and migration, the great blue heron is a solitary creature. Most of Pennsylvania's migratory great blue herons spend their winters in the Caribbean or in Central America (some do remain in the state year-round), then return to the same place to nest again, year after year. Males choose the nest sites, usually rebuilding and enlarging the same nest every spring. Constructed of sticks, the average nest is 3 to 4 feet in diameter and 30 to 40 inches across.

Both parents incubate the three or four pastel-blue eggs during the 28-day incubation period. They also share the feeding of their nestlings for the two months they spend in the nest and for the additional third month, in which the young explore the adjoining treetops by first hopping out of the nest and into nearby branches, then learning to use their bills as hooks and pulling themselves farther from their nests, branch by branch. When they are four months old they are on their own.

Their parents, in the meantime, have been busy feeding them regurgitated fish, first beak to beak and later by depositing it in the nest bottom for the young to pick up. The sanctuary herons get their fish from Pymatuning Lake, Shenango Reservoir, and the rivers and streams feeding into them, all within five miles of the sanctuary.

Because the keen-eyed observer with a spotting scope can easily watch the drama of a great blue heron colony from the shelter, an increasing number of visitors have been finding their way to the sanctuary, especially in the spring. Although visitors come from as far away as Sweden and Argentina, the majority are from Pennsylvania or nearby Ohio, and of those, most are local people—the volunteers and their guests—whose enthusiasm has made the Brucker Great Blue Heron Sanctuary of Thiel College the leading conservation group in the area.

To join the Brucker Great Blue Heron Sanctuary of Thiel College, write to the sanctuary at P.O. Box 362, Greenville, PA 16125, and request an application form. No contribution is required, but any donation to further education efforts on behalf of the herons is appreciated.

From Exit 1 of Interstate 80, Sharon: Follow Pa. 18 north 7.9 miles to Shenango Lake. Cross Shenango Lake (0.7 mile). Continue north on Pa. 18 for 4.2 miles until you see a large Agway mill on your left. Drive 0.2 mile farther, and you will see a sign on the right-hand side of the highway for "Brucker Sanctuary" with a left arrow. Because the highway is divided, you must continue north another 0.2 mile, where you can exit right onto Crestview Drive, cross the highway, and return (south) back to the road into the sanctuary on the west side of the highway. The sanctuary parking lot is about 200 feet from the highway.

39   FRENCH CREEK

The Nature Conservancy calls French Creek, in northwestern Pennsylvania, "one of the nation's remaining hotbeds of mussel diversity." A fish biologist found that French Creek contains the most diverse group of fish of all the stream systems he studied during a three-year statewide investigation of fishes and stream communities. Botanists are impressed by the diversity of plant life found along its banks, including several rare and endangered species in Pennsylvania. Birders are on the lookout for bald eagles, black terns, marsh wrens, and American and least bitterns.

In addition to having something for almost everyone interested in the natural world, French Creek, which meanders through portions of Erie, Crawford, Mercer, and Venango counties before emptying into the Allegheny River at Franklin, is also popular with fishers, canoeists, and even stream-waders—people who wade downstream for the sheer pleasure of it.

The best way to see French Creek is in a canoe. Because the creek is relatively shallow in places, canoeing is best done in the spring and early summer. In fact, "uncertain water levels" on the creek throughout the year helped to speed the demise of the Franklin Canal Company, which constructed a canal from the mouth of French Creek to the vicinity of Meadville in 1833. Remnants of the canal are still visible along stretches of French Creek, and its towpath continues to serve as the roadbed for the railroad. A nice stretch of the creek can be explored

View of French Creek. Jeremy Woodhouse, photographer.

by launching your canoe at the Conservancy's public access at Utica in Venango County.

The Western Pennsylvania Conservancy is especially interested in French Creek's ecological significance, including its 66 fish species, such as the rare Ohio lampreys, gravel chubs, redfin shiners, warmouths, mountain, brindled, and northern madtoms, and bluebreast, spotted, Tippecanoe, gilt, and longhead darters. Its 25 freshwater mussels, with such alluring names as snuffbox, purple wartyback, fatmucket, round pigtoe, plain pocketbook, and squawfoot, are also important. This unusual biodiversity could be threatened by runoff from roads and parking lots, siltation from farms and logged woodlands, and chemicals.

So far, though, Dr. David H. Stansbery of Ohio State University, who studied French Creek's mussels in 1988, believes only one species has been lost in the watershed. Because of degraded stream conditions elsewhere in Pennsylvania, seven of French Creek's mussel species should be classified as endangered in Pennsylvania, and of those the northern riffleshell, the club-shell, and the rayed bean are candidates for the federal endangered-species status.

You don't have to be a malacologist (mussel specialist) to be impressed by the sheer size and beauty of the thousands of mussels packed near the shore in the sandy riffles in many places. And you don't need to know their names to appreciate their varied sizes, shapes, and colors, which are almost as diverse as seashells—and no wonder, since they are descendants of marine ancestors that millions of years ago entered from coastal bays and estuaries and headed upstream into rivers and their tributaries.

Diverse mussel beds used to be common in the eastern watershed of the Mississippi, an area that once contained the world's greatest collection of freshwater mussels. But even as early as 1909, mussel expert A. E. Ortmann was writing: "The worst damage to our fauna is done by the pollution of the streams, . . . by sewage, . . . coal mines, . . . oil wells, . . . chemical factories, woodpulp mills, saw mills, tanneries, etc. [and] finally, . . . the damming up of certain rivers. . . . It is most destructive to mussels, most of which require a lively current." Also, according to present-day ecologists, mussels act like canaries in a coal mine because they eat by using their siphons to filter the water for food, so whatever chemicals and particulates there are in the water are deposited in their shells and flesh. Thus people interested in water quality have been able to trace toxic metals in mussels to the place that leaked them.

Not all of French Creek is pristine, but the area near Utica is especially healthy, a part of the lower portion between Carlton (Mercer County) and Sugar Creek (Venango County), which is considered one of the best stretches on the creek. But although it is a thrill to have a glimpse of rare mussel species, look for banks of handsome, waist-high ostrich ferns along the creek. Ostrich ferns produce the best of edible fiddleheads and are commercially harvested in Maine and Canada, then preserved by either canning or freezing. They are also one of our showiest ferns, their plumelike fronds growing as high as 10 feet in low, rich soil along rivers and streams. If you look carefully, you will find the stiff, dried, dark-brown, lyre-shaped fertile fronds of the previous year in the midst of the new green of the season's fronds. A few of the plants sharing the bank with the ostrich ferns are jack-in-the-pulpits, sensitive ferns, dame's rocket, and skunk cabbage.

During a late-spring canoeing trip, birding by ear is especially profitable. You might hear singing northern (Baltimore) orioles, red-eyed vireos, scarlet tanagers, song sparrows, black-billed cuckoos, great-crested flycatchers, hooded warblers, eastern wood pewees, wood thrushes, yellow warblers, and ruby-crowned kinglets. Even better, look for great blue herons lifting off ahead of you, eastern kingbirds sitting on snags, belted kingfishers emitting their rattling cries as they fly, green-backed herons probing in the shallows, and adult Canada geese with young foraging on the shore. I was even lucky enough to see, as I canoed on French Creek, a female common merganser carrying five young on her back, which I followed for a mile or more.

French Creek is the kind of place that requires slow paddling with many stops along the way to explore, and frequent back-paddling in pursuit of elusive bird calls, the perfect photograph, booming bullfrogs, or small fish. But taken at that pace, by the time you return to Utica you should be able to see why French Creek has such allure for a wide variety of outdoors people intent on appreciating nature.

From Pittsburgh: Take Interstate 79 north. At Exit 33, take U.S. 62 and follow it to Sandy Lake. Proceed north through the town and pick up Pa. 173 north toward Cochranton. After driving 4.4 miles beyond Sandy Lake, turn right on Georgetown Road. Continue for another 4 miles to a sign to Utica. Turn left there. Proceed 3 miles and follow the main street until it crosses French Creek. Turn left just beyond the bridge but before the railroad tracks, into the WPC-owned access.

40   CLEAR CREEK STATE FOREST / ALLEGHENY RIVER AREA

Most of Clear Creek State Forest, as well as Clear Creek State Park, is located in northern Jefferson and southern Forest counties. But in southern Venango County a 3,165-acre tract of Clear Creek State Forest includes six miles of frontage along the western shore of the Allegheny River.

In addition to the scenic six-mile-long River Trail, which parallels the Allegheny River, the forest's 20.5-mile trail system meanders up, over, and around the mountainous plateau area that looms above the river valley. For a relatively easy, four-mile loop through the most scenic and historically interesting section of the forest, begin at the gated dirt road labeled "River Trail." Follow the orange blazes that mark the Clear Creek State Forest trails.

During our visit in late October, most of the migrant bird species you might see here in the spring and summer, such as the hooded and black-and-white warblers, red-eyed vireos, and eastern wood pewees, were gone for the year. But resident black-capped chickadees and a pileated woodpecker noisily announced themselves along this portion of the trail. No doubt the many tree cavities in this area provide nesting and resident sites for those species.

On the steep bank to the left, large tulip trees and some cucumber magnolias grow in the mostly hemlock forest. Massive boulders support evergreen wood ferns, rhododendron shrubs, and common polypody. According to Boughton Cobb in his *Field Guide to the Ferns*, "Thoreau refers to the 'fresh and cheerful communities' of the Polypody in early spring." Furthermore, French Canadians call it *tripe de roche* because of its rich, lustrous, velvety, mantle-like growth over rocky surfaces. A small evergreen fern, it spreads itself like a heavy mat on top of boulders shaded by thick woods. There is also a lovely stand of maidenhair fern growing beside the trail.

Just over a mile beyond the starting gate, after the area to the right

Dennison Run. Clear Creek State Forest/Allegheny River Area.

widens out into a floodplain, you reach Dennison Run on the left. Turn left on the orange-blazed Dennison Run Trail, which parallels this "exceptional value stream," so classified because of its outstanding water quality. Remnant leaves of foamflowers and hepaticas are a sign that this area is a good place to find an abundance of spring-blooming wildflowers. Christmas ferns and New York ferns join the still abundant common polypody and evergreen wood ferns in this cool, shaded, mostly hemlock hollow with some sugar maple and American beech trees.

No sight or sound of humans reached us once we turned off onto Dennison Trail. All we heard was the rippling water of Dennison Run and occasional calls from downy woodpeckers, more chickadees, golden-crowned kinglets, white-breasted nuthatches, and dark-eyed juncos.

At about 0.8 mile along the Dennison Run Trail, turn left onto Iron Furnace Trail, and left again up the hillside paralleling a tributary of Dennison Run, following the faint white and orange blazes of Iron Furnace Trail. Between boulders in this picturesque, hemlock-enshrouded gorge, a couple of small, narrow waterfalls flow. The climb is gentle, but watch the blazes carefully until you reach a plateau. Not only does the landform change, but so does the forest, from mostly conifer to almost entirely deciduous and predominately large oak trees.

At a T-intersection, turn right, still on the orange-blazed Iron Furnace Trail. Or, if you want to add two more miles to the hike, take a left on Kennerdell Trail and another left on Lookout Trail to Dennison Point Lookout, which presents a scenic view of the Allegheny River 500 feet below and the wooded, seemingly uninhabited hills beyond. This over-look can also be reached halfway along the Dennison Run Trail by turning left onto Lookout Trail. Although this route to the lookout is considerably shorter, when we tried it we found it to be exceedingly steep and slippery, rising 400 feet in less than 0.4 mile. Still, for the adventurous and sure-footed, it can be done.

After the Kennerdell Trail branches off, the Iron Furnace Trail descends through another hemlock forest that is interspersed with occasional large white pine trees. Halfway down, notice a prominent sign to the left that says "Kennerdell." Continue straight ahead, still toward the iron furnace.

The remains of the furnace are heavily festooned with ferns, moss, tree saplings, wild grape vines, and wildflowers. According to the interpretive sign, the furnace, built in 1840, was probably active only about 10 years. But in those years 1,000 acres of the surrounding forest were clear-cut to produce the charcoal that in turn was used to produce three tons of pig iron each day it was in operation. Although the forest seems to have re-covered from the clear-cutting, the surrounding hills still bear visible scars from where the iron ore and slate were dug out in strips. In the spring, the winter's production of pig iron was floated down the Alle-gheny River on timber rafts to Pittsburgh.

The state forest brochure and trail map remind people that today "state forest land is managed under the multiple-use concept. Timber manage-ment and oil and gas operations are carried out under sound conserva-tion principles," unlike the period when the iron furnace was in opera-tion. Most of the oil and gas areas seem to be north of Dennison Run Trail, and we saw no evidence of recent timbering in the areas we hiked.

Retrace your steps uphill to the Kennerdell sign (South Trail) and turn right. In this area the oak trees are once again dominant, but hemlocks, the last in the succession of Pennsylvania forest tree species, form an understory 30 feet high. After a mile of meandering through the forest, still following orange blazes, the trail turns a sharp right for about one-tenth of a mile and then loops left, dipping steeply down to the road several hundred yards from the gated entrance to River Trail, where your car is parked. In this area, we missed the turns because the trail was poorly marked, and we ended up bushwhacking down to the road, but recently more work has been done on the fainter trails, which should help. Nevertheless, before visiting, you should call 814-226-1901 or write the DER Bureau of Forestry, 158 South Second Avenue, Clarion, PA 16214-1904, and ask for their trail guide and brochure for Clear Creek State Forest, Allegheny River Tract.

In addition to hiking, the forest is open for boating and fishing on the river, cross-country skiing and snowmobiling on specified trails in the winter, and camping. The Danner Camping Area, another mile beyond the Dennison Run Trail turnoff on River Trail, can be used as a stopover during float trips on the Allegheny River and can be reached by boating or hiking. Restrooms and water are available there. Backpack camping is also permitted on the state forest land, although you must move your camp each day.

From Exit 4 of Interstate 80: Follow Pa. 308 north 0.7 mile to the intersection at the center of Clintonville. Continue north on 308 another 3.1 miles and turn right onto a paved road marked by a sign for Kennerdell. Drive 4.3 miles on this road until the Allegheny River comes into view on the right, and park on the right in a pullout 0.3 mile farther, about 100 feet before the bridge across the river to Kennerdell. Directly beyond the bridge is a gated dirt road, the beginning of River Trail.

41   CLARION RIVER

Not many roadless areas exist along Pennsylvania's rivers, but the Clarion River from Cook Forest State Park to Piney Dam is as close as you can come to a wild, scenic river in Pennsylvania. That stretch has always been relatively untouched by the often heavy hand of humans. In fact, the entire westward-flowing river, with its headwaters in McKean County, has been the stuff of local poets ever since pioneers moved into the area near the end of the eighteenth century.

They did not call it the Clarion River, but either Toby's Creek or Stump

Canoeing on the Clarion River.

Creek. To the local Indians it was the Tobeco, and French explorers knew it as Rivière au Fiel. But one night in 1817, surveyors for a new state road stretching from Bedford in the south to Franklin in the north camped beside the Clarion. As they lay in their tent, they heard "the clear sound of the distant ripples," caused by the dense forest of giant trees that "condensed and reflected the murmur, giving it a silvery mellowness," according to A. J. Davis in his *History of Clarion County.* One surveyor, Daniel Stanard, commented that it sounded like the notes of a distant clarion. His assistant, David Lawson, suggested, "Why not call it the Clarion River?"—and the Clarion it became, despite old-timers who clung to the older names.

Although the giant trees were cut down when the rest of Pennsylvania was stripped, the 40-mile section of the river from Ridgway in Elk County to Piney Dam in Clarion remained relatively undeveloped. Much of the upper Clarion was protected by the Allegheny National Forest, state game lands, Kittanning State Forest, and Clear Creek and Cook Forest state parks. The rest was in private hands.

But despite the recovery of the riverbanks from logging, the condition of the river itself did not encourage recreational use. Polluted water flowed into it from paper mills and acid mine discharges, turning the river an unappetizing inky color and staining the rocks orange. It also smelled bad. Worst of all, there was no life in the river, not even stoneflies or caddisfly nymphs. In the 1960s, sections of the river had a pH of 4.0, far below the tolerance of any fish species.

So in 1976, when the late director of the Western Pennsylvania Conservancy, Roger Latham, recommended that they consider acquiring the middle section of the Clarion River corridor, no one else shared his enthusiasm—until he persuaded several Conservancy staff members to accompany him on a canoe trip down the Clarion.

To everyone's surprise, the river was not only wild and scenic but alive! Four-foot-long muskies, rainbow trout, and walleyes were reported from Cooksburg to Mill Creek. The Clarion River cleanup had been launched by state and federal government agencies, private industries, and many service clubs. Special credit was given to the DER's surface-mine reclamation program (Operation Scarface) on the Clarion's East Branch, as well as the cleanup of paper-mill waste above Ridgway. Impressed by what they had seen, the Conservancy began to acquire land along the Clarion River in 1976. Since then they have saved nearly 9,000 acres of shoreline, hillside, and island property.

In the spring a nice stretch of the river to canoe is from Cooksburg to Piney Dam—the only way to see the most pristine stretch of the Clarion. The old stands of hemlock and white pine intermingled with enormous oak trees on either side of the river once you leave Cooksburg behind are comparable to those the surveyors had found 173 years earlier. Swallows dip along ahead of you over the water, and great blue herons are abundant. No sound or sight of technology penetrates the almost primeval scene around you. Except during high water—the condition when we canoed the Clarion—this is canoeing for the novice, until you reach the rapids. Then, although the river's rating is Class C (flatwater), at least two rapids are rated Class I (high water) or Class II. Still, anyone equipped with a lifejacket should not hesitate to canoe in the Clarion River during warm weather.

A nice place to stop is at the stony beach at Maxwell Run, six miles from Cooksburg. There you can stretch your legs and take a short hike. With its lush greenery and variety of wildflowers, Maxwell Run invites exploration.

Then launch your canoe for the final 4.5-mile peaceful stretch, which echoes with birdsong—common yellowthroats, black-throated green warblers, scarlet tanagers, wood thrushes, yellow warblers, red-eyed vireos, black-capped chickadees, white-breasted nuthatches, black-and-white warblers. All will be disembodied voices, heard but not seen. You may be reminded of John Graves's classic *Goodbye to a River*, in which he wrote: "A river has few 'views.' It seeks the lowest line of its country, straight or crooked, and what you see when you travel along it are mostly sky and trees, water and clouds and sun and shore. Things a quarter-mile away exist for you only because you know they are there; your consciousness of them is visual only if you walk ashore to see them."

For this reason, frequent stops, such as that at Maxwell Run, are the order of the day. Unfortunately, the day we canoed the Clarion River it was raining hard, so it was difficult to stop as much as we would have liked. But although we would have preferred a sunny day on the river, the rain gave us a true wilderness experience. During the entire trip we saw no other person on the shore or on the river. We might almost have been French voyagers canoeing the Rivière au Fiel.

From Interstate 80: Take Exit 13, Brookville, onto Pa. 36 north. Drive approximately 17 miles to a bridge over the Clarion River. Immediately after crossing the bridge, turn right and look for the Cook Forest State Park office parking lot on the left. To your right is the river and put-in area.

42   PINE SWAMP NATURAL AREA

In early spring before the mosquitoes hatch, or in early fall after the first frost, Pine Swamp Natural Area in northwest Mercer County is at its most comfortable. But if you don't mind mosquitoes and do like high-bush blueberries, try midsummer. Whenever you choose to visit this 395-acre tract, be prepared to get wet knees, because Pine Swamp lives up to its watery name.

Purchased by the Western Pennsylvania Conservancy piecemeal between 1974 and 1981 because of its unique-to-western-Pennsylvania raised barren in the midst of the swamp, the natural area itself consists of three distinct sections: the raised peatland, the surrounding marsh,

Wetland at the Pine Swamp Natural Area.

and the swamp forest. A yellow-blazed trail through this almost-level terrain takes you to all three sections, although once the signed area is reached most of the walking is in the forest.

After parking, take the mowed path to the left of the pond, then cross the pipeline right-of-way to the sign that instructs you to proceed straight ahead into the natural area. For a short side-spur, look for a narrow side trail to the left that leads to a view of the open marsh, being careful to remain silent if you hope to glimpse such birds as great blue herons.

Retrace your steps back to the original natural-area sign and follow the main trail as it plunges into the high vegetation of an abandoned old field. Here it is buzzy with dragonflies and honeybees, the trail occasionally squishes underfoot, and, in early fall, color radiates from numerous species of goldenrod and asters. The bank of red-osier dogwood, with its white berries and scarlet stems, to the right, is particularly striking. Ruffed grouse explode from cover, gray catbirds "mew" in the underbrush, American goldfinches bounce above the fluttering monarch butterflies, and blue jays scream at the red-tailed hawk circling slowly in the open sky overhead.

From there the trail ascends to the swamp forest, where in autumn the hawthorn bushes are loaded with red haws, and large American beech trees drop an abundant crop of nuts. That was where we surprised a flock of wild turkeys foraging for beechnuts and, shortly afterward, an eight-point buck, which ran across the trail in front of us. Later, we also watched a fat woodchuck waddle slowly past us without a backward glance, and two does leap to their feet and bolt only when we passed within a few yards of their resting place. Wildlife appeared amazingly tame in Pine Swamp Natural Area, perhaps because people rarely visit swamps, which are often perceived as wet, buggy, inhospitable places.

Wildflowers too are abundant in the swamp forest. The parasitic beech-drop flowers cover the forest floor beneath the beech trees, and along a fork of Wolf Creek orange or spotted touch-me-nots blossom in company with the moisture-loving sensitive ferns. In the spring, white trillium, painted trillium, Canada mayflower, bloodroot, cut-leaved toothwort, spring beauty, hepatica, and trout-lily all grow beneath a canopy of red maple, eastern hemlock, white pine, and white oak trees, as well as the beech trees. The understory consists, in part, of mountain laurel, high-bush blueberry, and four species of viburnum: blackhaw, maple-leaf viburnum, wild-raisin, and hobblebush.

Eventually the trail reaches a view of Pine Swamp itself with its concentric marsh zone just outside the raised peatland, and you realize that what seems like a vast woods is actually an island surrounded by wetlands. The yellow-blazed trail keeps to the dry outer ring where gold-thread leaves and wintergreen cover the ground, and royal fern, cinnamon fern, violets, and mosses thrive on the hummocks surrounding the willow, spirea, and alder shrubs.

Farther out in the wet, spongy sphagnum mat grow Virginia chain fern, cotton grass (*Eriophorum virginicum*), marsh St. Johnswort, the tiny four-lobed, yellow-flowered bartonia with its wiry, leafless stem, wild cranberry, and the aquatic yellow or greater bladderwort. The latter, *Utricularia vulgaris,* has small yellow flowers reminiscent of butter-and-eggs sticking above the water, and threadlike leaves covered with tiny bladders under the water or buried in the mud. Like sundews, pitcher plants, and Venus flytraps, bladderworts are carnivorous plants, and the pinhead-sized bladders have lids that close on water insects like miniature trap doors.

On the raised barren itself is a scattering of quaking aspens, white pine and gray birch trees, nannyberry, and high-bush blueberry shrubs, all of which are dominated by a dense shrub layer of chokeberry. If you want to examine this area more closely, be prepared to sink knee-deep in the water surrounding the raised bog. I must confess that we stayed on dry ground and used our binoculars to good advantage, getting a feel for the beauty of the swamp but staying relatively dry.

As we gazed out over Pine Swamp, we felt as if we had. regressed millions of years. No human sounds interrupted our reverie, and it was easy to imagine some prehistoric dinosaur rising from the marsh, which seemed so primitive and untouched. Indeed, humanity has scarcely penetrated it. Only the swamp forest has been selectively logged at various times, leaving a mostly second-growth hemlock forest of dense quiet farther along the trail, with a thick ground cover of tree clubmoss (*Lycopodium obscurum*) and running pine clubmoss (*Lycopodium complanatum*), as well as partridgeberries. Here wood thrushes call, black-capped chickadees chatter as they forage among the hemlock cones, and downy woodpeckers tap on snags. The trail completes a circle in these woods, and it is essential to keep one eye on the yellow blazes, paying particular attention to the double blazes, which indicate a turn.

Eventually you will be retracing your steps, still on the yellow-blazed trail, and you should recognize a wooden bridge you crossed earlier in the hike. From there it is an easy half-mile back to your car through the woods and abandoned field. Should you get turned around for any reason, remember that Route 965 is due south.

Originally a by-product of the last glacial retreat in western Pennsylvania 20,000 years ago, when it once was a shallow, rain-filled lake that became the headwaters for both the westward flowing Fox Run and the southward flowing Wolf Creek, the Pine Swamp Natural Area gradually filled up with decayed vegetation over thousands of years. Although its physical character has changed through the centuries, its main water source—rainfall—has not. Neither has the direction of its two streams.

Such watery retreats are rare in the United States because so many wetlands have been drained for more ephemeral structures, such as shopping centers and housing developments. Luckily the Western Pennsylvania Conservancy has preserved this unique environment for generations of Pennsylvanians to enjoy "in the rough." Pine Swamp Natural Area offers serenity and solitude difficult to find in these harried, latter days of the twentieth century and should be visited as often as possible in order to observe the many birds, animals, wildflowers, and trees that call this place home.

From Pittsburgh: Take Interstate 79 north about 55 miles to Exit 33. Drive east for approximately 4 miles on U.S. 62 until it joins with Pa. 965. Continue straight ahead on Route 965 another 4 miles, and watch for a white house with a pond behind it, on the left side of the road. Park in the grassy area to the left of the house, being careful not to block either the garage doors or the nearby concrete-block building.

43   FRINGED GENTIAN FEN NATURAL AREA

September is the time to visit the Fringed Gentian Fen Natural Area east of New Castle in Lawrence County. The smallest holding of the Western Pennsylvania Conservancy, this 0.8-acre wetland has a variety of moisture-loving wildflowers that peak early in the month. Although the lovely dark-blue, fringed gentian is the stated feature of the area, a close look yields dozens of other attractive wildflowers as well.

But don't go unprepared. Wear high rubber boots and pants that can be rolled up, or if the day is warm enough, shorts and old sneakers. Pick a clear day, because fringed gentian flowers close up if even one cloud passes over the sun. And take along a good wildflower guide, because unless you are an expert botanist you will find at least a couple of new-to-you species.

The property is long and narrow with horses grazing at the far edge of the wetland. Dogs from neighbors on either side of the small natural area bark as you park the car beside the cable marker and descend a narrow trail down a close-cut green strip to the watery fen below.

A fen, like a bog, is a waterlogged area. But unlike bogs, which have no inflow or outflow of water and depend only on precipitation, a fen also receives surface and groundwater. As this water moves through and over the soil, it gathers and carries organic materials, dissolved minerals, and gases, which, if the water moves slowly, dissolves enough calcium to create a basic soil. Such a soil is favored by a large variety of shrubs, trees, and wildflowers.

The Fringed Gentian Fen Natural Area, at first glance, looks like an ordinary cattail marsh with numerous wildflowers both along its edges and growing in the wet ditches—not, by any stretch of the imagination,

View of the Fringed Gentian Fen Natural Area.

a wilderness area. But closer study reveals its plant diversity.

Gold and purple are the predominant wildflower colors, with green-headed coneflowers, bur-marigold, and several species of goldenrod in its upper reaches. Off to the sides are the enormously tall, reddish-purple, spotted Joe-Pye-weed and the more deeply purple New York ironweed, so-named because of its extremely tough stems. Both are showy members of the Composite family that are common indicators of a wetland. Although New York ironweed was considered a pest by farmers, Joe-Pye-weed, according to legend, was distributed in Salem, Massachusetts, by an Indian herbalist named Joe Pye as a cure for typhus.

It is easy to see all the large common wildflowers, but you must look down among the stems and grasses to find several of the less common species, such as the nodding ladies'-tresses, which has tiny white flowers growing in a double spiral along a short stem clasped by slender leaves at its base. Another, mostly white flower that prefers wet feet is the turtle-head, which has a cluster of swollen, two-lipped flowers at the tip of its one-to-three-foot stem. If you squeeze a blossom at its base, the "turtle" will open its mouth.

Nestled in the middle of the swamp are the distinctive arrow-shaped leaves of the aquatic broad-leaved arrowhead, although its showy, three-petaled white flowers are no longer in bloom by September. Still another hidden white wildflower is the grass-of-Parnassus, its five-petaled blossoms veined with green, looking more like a delicate wildflower of early spring than a robust fall blossom. A species found primarily in the Midwest, the only eastern state it reaches is Pennsylvania.

A few plants of great lobelia grow not far from the stream that forms the northern boundary of the natural area. Named *Lobelia siphilitica* because it was once thought to be a cure for syphilis, it has numerous bright-blue, tubular flowers with three downward-pointing lobes striped with white and two plain blue upward-pointing lobes growing out from the juncture of the stem and the leaf.

Finally, hidden off to one side of the trail, is the "heaven's own blue" of fringed gentian, as poet William Cullen Bryant called it. There may be no more than a handful of the two-inch-long bell-shaped flowers, each with four flaring fringed petals growing atop one-foot-high stalks. Because the fringed gentian is a true biennial, it takes two years to bloom, and then it dies. Unfortunately, it often grows in farm meadows that are cut during the summer. When this happens, still another stand of fringed gentian perishes because it has not had time to set seed. It also is fussy in its growing habits and needs a heavy amount of magnesium in the soil as well as a neutral pH of 7.0, difficult to find during these days of acid rain with a pH often as sour as vinegar at 4.0. The fen, however, with its alkaline soil is an excellent habitat for fringed gentian.

To discover even a small stand of fringed gentian today is a rare treat, even though it was once so common that it blanketed eastern meadows with a sheet of blue praised by poets and naturalists alike. Thoreau described the color as "such a dark blue!" and poet Emily Dickinson called it "a purple creature that ravished all the hill" with its "Tyrian" blue. But it was Bryant who immortalized it in his "To the Fringed Gentian," as a "sweet and quiet eye. . . . Blue—blue—as if that sky let fall / A flower from its cerulean wall."

What more could any wildflower enthusiast ask for than a crisp, clear fall day filled with all the brilliant colors of autumn flowers set off by a blue that inspired poems and essays in its praise?

From Interstate 79: Take Exit 30 and turn west on Pa. 108 toward New Castle. After 7.8 miles, take a left onto Pa. 388. Drive another 1.6 miles, then turn right onto Frew Mill Road. Proceed 0.4 mile until you see an orange AT&T cable marker number 106 on the left, which marks the beginning of the fen. Park along the side of the road.

44   MORAINE STATE PARK AND MILLER ESKER NATURAL AREA

Fourteen thousand years ago, two enormous lakes dominated the landscape in northwestern Butler County. Now known as Lake Arthur and Lake Edmund, they were both formed when the eastern edge of the Wisconsin Ice Sheet dammed Slippery Rock and Muddy creeks and flooded their valleys with glacial meltwater and runoff. Lake Edmund, to the north and east of Lake Arthur, was the larger and higher of the two lakes, and its water flowed into Lake Arthur over a narrow spillway. Lake Arthur's water escaped over a waterfall into what is now called Stony Run.

Then the temperatures rose, the glacier melted, and many outlets to the south of the lakes opened up, causing the lakewaters to flood south. So powerful were those floodwaters that they gouged out nearby McConnells Mill Gorge in less than 100 years. This newly created gorge permanently reversed the flow of water in the area, and instead of moving north into the St. Lawrence River the streams flowed south into the Ohio River watershed.

Lake Edmund disappeared forever with the melting of the glacier, but a portion of Lake Arthur was re-created in 1970 when a dam was built on Muddy Creek, once again flooding the Muddy Creek valley. This time, though, Lake Arthur was smaller—7 instead of 13 miles long, and elevated to 1,190 feet rather than 1,260 feet—but today, at 3,225 acres, it is still the largest man-made state-owned lake entirely within Pennsylvania's borders. In addition, surrounding the lake are the 16,000 acres of Moraine State Park forestland, which makes the park one of the commonwealth's largest.

Created in a valley still infertile because of its stony, glacial soil, the park was named for that soil or ground moraine deposited by the glacier. Building the dam to reflood a portion of Muddy Creek valley, though, was the last part of a project that included purchasing many parcels of land that had been heavily mined for their coal, gas, and oil deposits.

Flowering dogwood trees in bloom along the Sunken Garden Trail. Moraine State Park.

Acid mine drainage polluted many of Muddy Creek's feeder streams. Not only did the streams have to be cleaned up before the creek was dammed, but deep mines had to be sealed, strip mines backfilled and graded, and 422 gas and oil wells plugged.

While the Western Pennsylvania Conservancy purchased most of the initial land, the former Pennsylvania Department of Mines and Mineral Industries, and the Pennsylvania Department of Forests and Waters, cooperated to reclaim that land. Continuing its interest in conserving remnants of western Pennsylvania's last Ice Age, the Conservancy also purchased, and still owns, the Miller Esker Natural Area, north of Moraine State Park. So today it is possible to spend time exploring both areas with a geological eye on their past and a natural eye on their present.

The first place to stop is the Pleasant Valley Picnic Area at the park, where you can take the mile-long, circular Sunken Garden Trail on the south shore of Lake Arthur. During the mid-May day of our visit, we were met by a cascade of birdsong (yellow warblers, common yellowthroats, northern [Baltimore] orioles) and the quacking of mallard ducks as we emerged from our car and followed the walk signs across the field to a cattail marsh framed by half a dozen shagbark hickory trees. Early morning bird-watchers also claim that this wet area attracts great blue herons, swamp sparrows, green-backed herons, belted kingfishers, and Virginia rails.

After crossing the second footbridge over the marsh, turn right uphill into a pine woods and then continue through an overgrown field. Highlighted by dozens of flowering dogwoods and four redbud trees, on a spring day the field reverberates with the singing and calling of gray catbirds, song sparrows, northern cardinals, indigo buntings, and blue jays. Once you reach the scenic overlook of Lake Arthur, field plants and birds are replaced by water-loving ones. Pairs of Canada geese followed by downy goslings are common, and along the lakeshore sedges and wild irises thrive.

When you complete the circuit, proceed to the second short trail on the south shore of the lake, the Hilltop Nature Trail, by turning right after leaving the Pleasant Valley Picnic Area and following the park road for 1.7 miles until you reach the trail on the right. Much of this trail, like the Sunken Garden Trail, has been built on reclaimed strip-mined land and is interesting for that reason. Again, part of it is an overgrown field with some young woods, but it features black locust and pine trees, which in turn host American goldfinches, rufous-sided towhees, scarlet tanagers, yellow-breasted chats, white-eyed vireos, prairie warblers, and wood thrushes. The trail guide available at the park office will help you decide whether to follow the Short Loop (45 minutes long) or the Long Loop (1 hour, 15 minutes).

From there, return to U.S. 422 and turn left toward Butler. After three miles take the Prospect exit, turning left (north) on Pa. 528. Drive 4.4 miles and then turn left onto Lindey Road, continuing two miles until you reach a T-intersection, where you turn left. After 1.6 miles, turn left to park just before a steep, rock-strewn hill.

Walk down that hill and turn right onto the blue-blazed Glacier Ridge Trail. This heavily wooded area north of Lake Arthur is a showplace of spring wildflowers—yellow violets, mayapples, cut-leaved toothwort, rue anemone, Solomon's seal, jack-in-the-pulpit, white trillium, trout-lily, wild geranium, Canada mayflowers, and long-spurred violets. Altogether, the Glacier Ridge Trail stretches seven miles—from the Jennings Environmental Education Center at the junction of Pa. 8, 528, and 173, to the Davis Hollow Marina at the park. The mile-long section we walked is seductively beautiful and peaceful—and it is difficult to turn back, so if you have more time it is worthwhile to continue until your time runs out.

To visit the Miller Esker Natural Area, return to the T-intersection and continue straight ahead. After 0.2 mile, turn left onto a gravel road and then right on Roher Road after 0.6 mile. At a stop sign 0.6 mile farther, turn left. Drive 2.5 miles until you see a house on the left and a barn on the right. After another 0.1 mile, cross Swope Road and continue another 0.1 mile to where a line of woods meets an open field on the right. Park and follow that woods line, crossing a stream and proceeding straight up what looks like a long, low hill but is an esker.

Locally known as the West Liberty "hogback," this three-mile-long mound was constructed of sand and gravel deposited in a tunnel made by the glacier's meltwaters. Although part of the esker has been quarried, the Conservancy owns this entirely preserved, half-mile-long, 360-foot-wide and 40-foot-high portion. You can walk left (northwest) along its top until you reach the second lone tree in the field at the esker's left base. To the right, look over at Tamarack Lake (originally a glacier-formed kettlehole) and its wetland. Either retrace your steps on top of the esker, or follow it at its base back through the field, staying close to the mound. Both bobolinks and barn swallows are commonly seen coursing over the field in the spring.

While the Miller Esker Natural Area has much for people with an interest in geology, Moraine State Park appeals to a diverse cross-section of Pennsylvanians. On any lovely day Lake Arthur is filled with boating enthusiasts operating canoes, kayaks, rowboats, sailboats, and small motorboats. Fishers search for the northern pike, walleye, largemouth bass, tiger muskellunge, black crappies, and channel catfish stocked by the Pennsylvania Fish and Boat Commission. From Memorial Day until Labor Day, two beaches are available for swimming, and 1,200 picnic tables provide do-it-yourself meal facilities. Along Lake Arthur's northern shore, hikers on the Glacier Ridge Trail and bicyclists taking the paved, seven-mile-long bicycle trail can carry their own food or stop at the Marina Restaurant near the Davis Hollow Marina.

Winter is a popular season at Moraine State Park. Ice-skating, cross-country-skiing, ice-boating, ice-fishing, snowmobiling, sledding, and taking winter nature hikes are favorite activities. First proposed by the Western Pennsylvania Conservancy as a water-based recreation area back in 1951, Moraine State Park and its nearby environs have evolved not only to fill the need for outdoor recreation close to an urban population, but also to educate people about the glacial past of northwestern Pennsylvania.

From Pittsburgh: Take Interstate 79 north to Exit 29. Turn on U.S. 422 east and drive for just over 2 miles until you reach a left turn into the park heading toward the Pleasant Valley Picnic Area. Stop at the park office for maps. Then continue straight ahead for about 0.7 mile and turn right into the Pleasant Valley Picnic Area Boat Rental to walk the Sunken Garden Trail.

45   ELK-WATCHING

Twice, back in the 1980s, I roused myself at three in the morning and accompanied a knowledgeable elk aficionado north to elk country. Despite spending hours on foot and in the car at such popular elk-gathering spots as Winslow Hill, we neither saw nor heard them.

Then I learned about Parker Dam State Park's one-of-a-kind interpretive elk-watching program. Located in Clearfield County, Parker Dam State Park is half an hour south of sections in Elk and Cameron counties where wild elk roam. That population, recently censused at 205 animals, is one of two east of the Mississippi River (the other is in Michigan's Upper Peninsula).

Although the original eastern elk subspecies—*Cervus elaphus canadensis*—was extirpated in Pennsylvania during the latter part of the nineteenth century, between 1913 and 1926 Rocky Mountain elk (*C.e. nelsoni*) were stocked in several areas of the commonwealth. Only those in Elk and Cameron counties survived. The elk-watching program at Parker Dam State Park is offered biweekly from Memorial Day to Labor Day, and then once a month the rest of the year. Because each trip is limited to 20 participants, in order to provide a quality experience, it is wise to call the park office at 814-765-0630 several months ahead to sign up.

Park ranger Chip Harrison is in charge of the program, aided and abetted by his father Ralph. The senior Harrison, now retired from the Bureau of Forestry office in Emporium, has spent a lifetime keeping track of Pennsylvania's elk herds. Both men have helped Pennsylvania Game Commission employees with darting and radio-collaring selected elk. "We have been with the elk all our lives," Chip explained during one of his short talks to elk-watch participants.

Before every program, Ralph Harrison scopes out elk locations so both men have an idea of where the herds are. That knowledge, plus the time

Bull elk grazing in the winter along Pa. Route 555 between Benezette and Grant.

of year, dictates the meeting time and the places participants will visit. It is also the key to the program's success.

For a family outing in midwinter, sign up for the late January trip. You will be warned that you have only a fifty-fifty chance of seeing any of the animals. Winter outings require that you be at the park office by 7:00 A.M. Early morning is the best time to see elk at that time of year because you can get close to the animals.

People of all ages and walks of life show up for the outing and follow Chip northward in a caravan of vehicles. As you near elk territory, the day dawns, and you stop near Benezette to pick up Ralph Harrison, who is armed with the latest elk location data. On the day we visited, all the elk sightings were made along Pa. Route 555 between Benezette and Grant, even though we did try the Winslow Hill area too.

But we did see plenty of elk. First we made a quiet stop near the Grant area and walked along the road while Chip pointed out a few elk from the so-called Grant Group wandering wraithlike through the open woods across the way. The elk seemed unhurried and unconcerned by our silent watching and the clicking of cameras. That sighting was the wildest of the day, reminiscent of what Pennsylvania elk, rumored to be unusually large, must have looked like before human settlement and persecution had wiped them out.

The other sightings were in open meadows close to the road where bulls grazed like domestic cattle. Bull elk do not lose their antlers until April, so it was easy to distinguish them from the cows and calves.

To enrich the elk-watching experience, Chip gives participants plenty of information about elk natural history, management goals, and the ongoing efforts by the Game Commission and the Bureau of Forestry to provide ideal elk habitat on public lands. He also stresses proper elk-watching etiquette: maintaining a safe distance between the viewer and the elk, and not disrupting their activity. In addition, he demonstrates how the radio collars work. Altogether, the outing provides a well-rounded elk-watching program that everyone can enjoy no matter what their age or interests.

By the end of the trip I was hooked, and like many elk-watch participants I became a repeater. Although I was not able to make the end of June trip—the best time to see cows and calves still on their calving grounds—I did join the mid-September elk watch, which is potentially the most exciting watch of the year.

So it was! Despite the heavy rains all day, we met at the office at 5:00 P.M. The group was smaller—13 adults—and the ride much longer. After driving for an hour over progressively more rugged and remote back roads, the rain petered out just as our caravan of high-clearance vehicles reached the worst of the mud-slicked, puddle-filled state forest roads. We eased our trucks through the water and slid our way steadily uphill, stopping once to let four wild turkeys cross in front of us. By then most of us were having a hard time believing we were still in Pennsylvania, especially when we parked, started walking silently behind the Harrisons, and heard the electrifying bugling of a bull elk.

Slowly we advanced toward the sound, hugging the cover at the side of the road. Straining our eyes in the gray, still-dripping woods, we finally spotted elk moving across the road in front of us. We paused for many minutes until the Harrisons decided the elk had moved on. Then they motioned us forward.

Eventually we emerged into the open and saw a herd of cows, accompanied by at least two bulls, in the distance. They were grazing on a state-maintained meadow with a spectacular view. Binoculars were needed for a close look, and we passed ours around. But it was obvious the herd did not know we were there.

We turned up a side trail paralleling the meadow, still savoring the sight of wild elk against a backdrop of Pennsylvania mountains. Ralph Harrison, in the lead, suddenly gestured excitedly and pointed. Everyone stood spellbound as we watched something no elk-watch group had ever seen before: A bull elk was polishing his antlers on a sturdy sapling. Despite the distance, we could both hear his loud grunts and see what he was doing. To cap the experience, a rainbow appeared opposite a scarlet and purple sunset that lit up the western horizon. Towhees called, crickets chirped, and still that elk pushed and grunted.

And then the spell was broken. A herd of deer, looking like toy animals next to the massive elk, detected our presence and alerted the elk by fleeing. As the deer bounded off to the east, the elk streamed westward. In a few moments the meadow was empty. All of us were thrilled by what we had witnessed. The bugling—which ordinarily would have been the high point of our trip—had been upstaged by a much rarer sight.

Such then is the lure of Parker Dam State Park's unique program. No matter what the time of year, you have a chance not only to see elk but also to take away exciting memories that will last a lifetime.

If you want to see elk on your own, stop by the Parker Dam State Park office and pick up a copy of their "Self-Guided Elk-Watching" brochure, which includes an excellent map and directions to the primary viewing areas. Folks at the office may also be able to give you an idea of where the elk are likely to be.

From Interstate 80: To reach Parker Dam State Park, take Exit 18, Penfield, which is about 9 miles west of Clearfield, and follow Pa. 153 north 5.2 miles. Turn right onto a paved road at a prominent sign for Parker Dam State Park. Follow this road for 2.3 miles and stop at the park office on the right.

46   RACHEL CARSON HOMESTEAD AND TRAIL

A soft-spoken lady scientist from Springdale, Pennsylvania, tried to change the world more than three decades ago. In 1962 her book, *Silent Spring,* forever altered people's attitudes about the indiscriminate use of chemicals. Considered one of the most influential books of the twentieth

Rachel Carson's home. Rachel Carson Homestead.

century, along with Aldo Leopold's *Sand County Almanac*, Rachel Carson's *Silent Spring* continues to offer both a warning about where our excesses may lead us and hope that we might find our way before it is too late.

The call to write *Silent Spring* came in a letter from one of Carson's friends, Olga Owens Huckins. Olga and her husband owned a small place in Duxbury, Massachusetts, where they had created a bird sanctuary. Then the state began aerial spraying of DDT to control mosquitoes, telling nearby residents it would be no more than a "harmless shower." Immediately the Huckins's birds started dying. Frustrated by state officials who refused to change their policies, Olga Huckins wrote to Carson, who had once worked at the U.S. Fish and Wildlife Service, for help from the proper federal authorities.

Carson, in her thorough, scientific manner, began investigating for herself. The more she learned about chemical abuses, the more horrified she became. She realized that humans were tinkering more destructively than ever with the natural world and that all she loved was at stake.

It took her four years to marshal all her facts and write a literate account of pesticide use that Supreme Court Justice William O. Douglas called "the most important chronicle of this century for the human race." Vilified by chemical and agricultural interests, and praised by conservationists and a large segment of the scientific community, her conclusions about chemical abuse were vindicated by President John F. Kennedy's Science Advisory Committee report. Shortly afterward, Carson died of cancer in 1964.

Writing about pesticides was not a job Rachel Carson had undertaken lightly. She preferred to write about her beloved sea and had produced three classic books (*Under the Sea Wind, The Edge of the Sea,* and *The Sea Around Us*) before writing *Silent Spring*. She was a child of the Allegheny hills of western Pennsylvania, not "a child of the sea." Born on May 27, 1907, she had a modest home tucked amid 65 rural acres of woods and hills just north of Pittsburgh, but today the house is in a busy neighborhood in Springdale. Her father long ago sold the land for lots, to pay household bills, and the two ruts up the steep hill she knew have been transformed into a busy, paved street. But the house remains, set back on a large, wooded tract and identified by a small sign hanging just outside the wooden fence on 613 Marion Avenue.

Twice I have made a pilgrimage to Carson's home in an effort to get a feel for how her rural Western Pennsylvania roots might have influenced her love for the natural world. Owned and operated by the Rachel Carson Homestead Association since 1975, the two-story white-clapboard house has been partially renovated. Now it has both indoor plumbing and water, features it did not possess when Carson lived there. The house is also minimally furnished with the kind of furniture the Carsons might have owned. Memorabilia relating to Carson are on display, and visitors can tour the rooms and view a slide show about her life. The grounds outside, complete with a labeled wildflower garden, are also open to the public.

Recently the first phase of a master planning process begun in 1991 resulted in a new drawing of the restored homestead. In addition, the Homestead Association set two goals: "To fully restore the birthplace and early home of Rachel Carson and to develop educational programs based on her life and career." As a member of the Rachel Carson Homestead Association, I am kept informed by *Update*, a publication reporting the activities of the association. For instance, every May, Rachel Carson Day is celebrated in a unique way, related to her interest in the environment.

Springdale itself also benefits from the Rachel Carson Homestead Association. Every summer, local schoolchildren attend a nature program called "Wonder Week," which uses the Homestead grounds to learn about the connections between people and the natural world and strongly emphasizes the respect for life that Rachel Carson espoused. Even back in the 1950s, Carson recognized that educating the young was essential in any effort to change people's attitudes toward nature, so she wrote the lavishly illustrated *The Sense of Wonder*. Based on her own experience as a surrogate mother for her grandnephew Roger, that book is a primer for parents on how to imbue youngsters with a love of the natural world.

After spending an hour or two at the Rachel Carson Homestead you can drive to Crouse Run, a favorite spot of Rachel's, which she reached by trolley, often spending a free day there studying its natural history. Today Crouse Run forms a small portion of the 33-mile-long Rachel Carson Trail, which was conceived, developed, and continuously maintained by the Pittsburgh Council of the American Youth Hostels (AYH). The trail is blazed throughout its length by "traffic yellow" paint—the eastern portion with two-by-six-inch rectangles, the western part with small yellow circles. According to an AYH brochure, "the trail is rerouted as necessary due to development and the changing ownership of property."

You will soon agree with the AYH statement that "the trail is relatively primitive and is steep in places. No bridges have been built; so streams have to be crossed as is." Thus you may find yourself searching for trail signs, climbing steep, slippery banks, and fording Crouse Run. If you visit in autumn, look also for evidence of spring wildflowers in the form of leaves, notably those of wild geranium, Solomon's seal, several species of violets, and wild ginger, along with a medley of blooming early autumn flowers, including blue lobelias and green-headed coneflowers. Crouse Run and its banks are studded with saucer-sized fossiliferous rocks, evidence of the 310-million-year-old plants and animals that once lived in the area.

Best of all are the trees: stately sycamores with their blotchy, flaking, white and clay-yellow bark, growing on the floodplain, and enormous hemlocks that shade the deep ravines leading down into Crouse Run. Sitting in the silent shade of the hemlocks, you can imagine the lure Crouse Run had had for Carson. Perhaps it was there that she first conceived an inkling of what she later called "A Statement of Belief": "The pleasures, the values of contact with the natural world are, . . . available to anyone who will place himself under the influence of a lonely mountaintop—or the sea—or the stillness of a forest; or who will stop to think about so small a thing as the mystery of a growing seed."

The Rachel Carson Homestead is open to the public on weekends, but because of limited staffing a call well ahead of your trip is advisable. Tours can be arranged on other days by advance reservation (two weeks notice). Groups of 10 or more should give advance notice for any day of the week. There is a small admission charge. Call 412-274-5459 for further information or reservations. To receive a brochure on the Rachel Carson Trail, contact AYH Publications, 6300 Fifth Avenue, Pittsburgh, PA 15232. For $4.00 plus $1.00 postage and 6% sales tax, you can also obtain *A Hiker's Guide to the Rachel Carson Trail*, which includes a section-by-section trail description, a set of topographic maps, information on the use and history of the trail, and general hiking tips. The Western Pennsylvania Conservancy also provides a one-page guide for a Rachel Carson Trail hike that includes the Crouse Run section. Call 412-288-2777 for more information.

From Pittsburgh: Follow Pa. 28 north to the Harmarville Exit. From there turn onto Pa. 910 south and drive about 300 yards to Old Route 28. Turn left and follow it north through Harmarville and Cheswick and into Springdale. In Springdale, turn left on Colfax Street. Follow Colfax uphill to Marion Avenue. Turn right onto Marion. The homestead is in the middle of the first block on the left, at 613 Marion.

To drive to the Rachel Carson Trail, return to Pa. 28 and follow it south 11 miles to the intersection with Pa. 8 in Etna. Take Pa. 8 north, passing the intersection of Harts Run Road after 5.9 miles, and turn left on Craighead Road 0.7 mile farther. Drive 0.2 mile and turn left at the North Hills Church of the Nazarene.

Go 0.4 mile and turn right onto Sample Road. Proceed 0.7 mile on Sample Road, cross Crouse Run, and park on the left. The Carson Trail leads up Crouse Run to the north (right side) of Sample Road.

47   BOG PATH AND BOULDER TRAIL

Until 1898 the Appalachian Plateau in Ogle Township, Somerset County, was an old-growth forest. Dominated by eastern hemlocks, the 2,500-foot-high plateau also supported such hardwoods as sugar maple, American beech, red oak, and black cherry. But when the entire area was clear-cut by the Babcock Lumber Company between 1898 and 1913, it irrevocably changed the character of the land.

The brushy growth, which quickly enveloped the slash-covered earth, easily ignited from lightning strikes, man-made fires, and sparks thrown by the railroad, so most of the area burned over in the 1920s and 1930s. Then the denuded land had most of its topsoil washed into the streams and lowlands, exposing the underlying rock-rubble in many places. Poorly drained areas became so saturated with water that tree regeneration was retarded, and in the wettest places, bogs and wetland shrubs permanently replaced the forest. In the pockets of soil that remained, sun-tolerant species eventually regenerated.

Today the Babcock Division of the Gallitzin State Forest has developed the Bog Path, the Boulder Trail, and the J. P. Saylor Trail through the plateau area. Without the Interpretive Guide to the Bog Path Educational Trail provided by the state forest, most visitors would not realize the changes that humans have imposed on the landscape.

Except for the intrusive noise from trucks laboring up the mountain on nearby Route 56, the Bog Path, Boulder Trail, and their environs seem timeless. Because of its elevation and weather patterns, the plateau is colder and its growing season is shorter than the area immediately to the east. When we visited on an early September day, the air had the briskness of October, and the tree leaves had already begun to turn color.

Rhododendron growing in Wolf Rocks. Bog Path and Boulder Trail.

From the parking lot, follow the yellow and red blazes of the Bog Path, crossing the J. P. Saylor Trail after about 1,500 feet and then continuing southwest on the Bog Path for another 2,000 feet. At that point the path divides, and you should continue on the right fork 3,000 feet farther. Huge beds of clubmosses blanket the understory in many places, along with clumps of New York, cinnamon, interrupted, and bracken ferns. Blue jays, black-capped chickadees, and American goldfinches forage and call. Small plank bridges cross flowing springs, and in the clear water of one spring I spotted an enormous crayfish, which quickly buried itself in the detritus when I bent for a closer look. In a grove of maturing hemlock trees, I found both worm-eating and magnolia warblers.

The Bog Path itself is circular, but instead of continuing on around it, proceed straight ahead, following the yellow-blazed Boulder Trail to Wolf Rocks. Along the right side of the trail is a sizable boulder field encircled by clubmosses growing in the soil-filled crevices. The rocks themselves have been softened in many places by a mossy green blanket. Turkey vultures glide low over the boulders, and common ravens croak overhead. The landscape is strewn with the remains of old hemlock logs, and in some areas hemlocks have reseeded. That day the rhododendron, also common along the trail, provided attractive cover for a dark-eyed junco family, whose young were still sporting mottled upper breasts instead of the clear white of adults.

Finally Boulder Trail intercepts the J. P. Saylor Trail. Turn right on that trail to explore Wolf Rocks, a huge complex of boulders piled one on another, which creates numerous caves and crevices to entice the adventurous. While there is no sign of litter along either the Bog Path or Boulder Trail, Wolf Rocks shows evidence of numerous parties and rock-painting visitors—the latter eager to leave their names and "art work" as proof of their visit. Still, the clumps of woodland ferns and seedling rhododendron that seem to grow out of the rocks themselves add a picturesque note to the scene. You can also stop there to sit and eat a trail lunch before retracing your steps back along the Boulder Trail until you reach the Bog Path again.

Turn right to complete that loop trail. This section of the Bog Path gives visitors a good view of the bog studded with cotton grass—not a true grass, but a sedge topped by clusters of white, fluffy hairs reminiscent of cotton, hence also its alternate name: bog cotton. Water oozes from abundant sphagnum mosses, while the drier hillocks are luxuriantly covered by interrupted ferns. The wet center of the bog is crowded with cattails.

A closer look at the sphagnum areas should reveal the round-leaved sundew *Drosera rotundifolia*. Each plant has a rosette of small round leaves growing close to the ground, and each leaf has its own slender stalk and is covered with reddish glandular hairs. From June to August a one-sided cluster of inconspicuous white or pink flowers that open one at a time grows on the flower stalk overtopping the distinctive leaves. The hairy leaves exude a sticky juice that entraps unwary insects, the chief food of this carnivorous plant. Once the insect is caught, the plant folds its sticky leaf around its prey and digests it. Then the leaf unfurls and the glandular hairs fold back, ready to capture its next victim.

Nodding ladies'-tresses (*Spiranthes cernua*) is another abundant, fall-blooming wildflower in the bog area. The shiny, dark, clover-shaped evergreen leaves of still a third wetland wildflower species—goldthread—is the only above-ground evidence of this May to July blooming wildflower, but it is named for its bright yellow "roots," easily seen just below the ground surface.

A short boardwalk takes visitors across the wettest areas to the viewing tower, from which we watched a large flock of cedar waxwings eating the remnants of the low-bush blueberry crop, while a white-tailed deer posed quietly in the background. Standing there, you seem to be removed more than ever from civilization. But in reality it is only a short walk back to the parking lot, retracing the beginning 3,500-foot section you walked in on.

From Johnstown: Follow Pa. 56 south toward Bedford. Drive 9.7 miles beyond the intersection with U.S. 219, turn right onto Shade Road, and immediately right again into the parking lot.

48   POWDERMILL NATURE RESERVE AND LINN RUN STATE PARK

Research is what Powdermill Nature Reserve is all about. As the field station of Pittsburgh's Carnegie Museum of Natural History, this 2,200-

Adam Falls. Linn Run State Park.

acre property in the midst of the Laurel Highlands has a mixed habitat of woodlands, old fields, ponds, streams, and thickets. Such an environment is attractive to the many species of birds and mammals that are necessary to fuel the two major, ongoing projects at the reserve: bird-banding and mammalian ecology and physiology.

But in June 1983 this premier research facility decided to invite the public to enjoy at least a portion of the natural area, so they opened the newly constructed Florence Lockhart Nimick Nature Center, with its Rea Natural History Exhibit presenting the four ecosystems of the area, research at the reserve, and the archaeology of prehistoric Western Pennsylvania, as well as a videotape on Powdermill.

Two years later, the major Black Birch Trail—with shorter, adjoining trails—was completed through the rich woodlands and floodplain along Powdermill Run beginning at the right of the parking area beside the nature center. Because of its southern location, the Powdermill Nature Reserve is a meetingplace of many southern and northern bird and wildflower species. But during a visit in late April you might see a yellow-throated warbler, considered a common breeder in the southern and central United States but only a casual visitor farther north, singing from the top of a hemlock tree. Tucked among the more-common-to-Pennsylvania spring wildflower species along the Black Birch Trail is the attractive yellow-colored, halberd-leaved violet, as well as the five-petaled white-blossomed mountain anemone, both southern wildflower species. Two other species of anemone—wood and rue—also grow in that area, along with both the large-flowered (white) and red trilliums and two blue phloxes: *Phlox subulata* and *Phlox divaricata*.

If you are an avid birder, Powdermill Nature Reserve has a special allure during all seasons of the year. Unlike most bird-banding stations, which operate only during spring and fall migrations, the reserve bands the entire year under the direction of bird-bander Bob Leberman, author of the authoritative *Birds of Ligonier Valley*. Once an hour, six days a week, Leberman and his staff (many of whom are volunteers) check the mist nets, which are suspended between poles along a defined set of trails, for trapped birds and carefully extricate each bird. Some, such as the wood warblers and kinglets, are placid and easy to remove, but others—chickadees, tufted titmice, blue jays—are feisty and need a lot of patience, and tough fingers inured to sharp nips, to untangle. Each bird is then popped into its own disposable brown paper bag, which is clipped shut with a clothespin and taken to the lab. There the bird is weighed, measured, sexed, aged, checked for parasites, banded, and finally released through an open window.

Some 10,000 to 14,000 birds a year are handled, and by the end of 1990 more than 300,000 birds of some 150 species had been banded at Powdermill, with 60,000 reported retrievals of those birds. One, a Swainson's thrush, was shot in northeastern Peru. Another, a cedar waxwing banded in late summer at Powdermill, was found in Mexico City that winter, the first of its species ever recovered south of the United States border. So banding does tell researchers something about where birds go during the winter. It is also helpful for establishing longevity records, breeding history, fidelity to territory, and other behavioral characteristics.

Located in the path of a heavily traveled flyway, Powdermill is flooded with a wide variety of land-bird species during migration. One record to be proud of is that more of the diminutive ruby-crowned kinglets are banded at Powdermill than at any other spot in the nation—a record-breaking 100 between 1961 and 1965.

On the overcast April 30 morning that we watched researchers band, there seemed to be innumerable blue jays, most of which had half-fought their way out of the paper bags before they were opened. In addition to the more ordinary brown-headed cowbirds, chipping sparrows, dark-eyed juncos, tufted titmice, and rufous-sided towhees, they also turned up a hooded warbler, a pine siskin, a red-bellied woodpecker, and best of all, an immature orchard oriole. The latter stumped most of the birders watching, because instead of the usual rich black and chestnut-brown of the male orchard oriole, the immature looked like a warbler, because of its golden breast and black throat.

Holding each bird in your hand is bound to make you a better birder, because you can learn all the fine identifying characteristics that are never obvious during a quick look in the field. Even in the short time we observed the work we could see how quickly data accumulated. For instance, the large numbers of blue jays were *not* all the same. Their weight varied considerably, and so did their personalities. The late author Michael Harwood once wrote in *The Living Bird Quarterly*, "The behavior of individuals varies within species as well. . . . A catbird is more than a catbird in some respects; it is itself." That curiosity, about individual birds and about species as a whole, is no doubt what keeps bird-banders going, despite the often grueling pace they must set, especially during migration.

If you visit the reserve in winter, you might be able to persuade Dr. Joseph Merritt, director of Powdermill and author of the *Guide to the Mammals of Pennsylvania*, or one of his assistants, to show you his outdoor shrew traps and some of the live shrews he is studying in the laboratory. Short-tailed shrews are the major focus of Dr. Merritt's research on small-mammal winter survival adaptations, not only because they are common but also because they remain active throughout the winter.

How then do they survive the cold so well? By live-trapping shrews and examining them, Dr. Merritt has determined that short-tailed shrews have a variety of methods for coping with winter temperatures. They singly occupy a well-insulated nest, hoard food such as beechnuts, forage in the comparatively warmer leaf litter zone beneath the snow, reduce their activity during intense cold, and produce internal heat through their own body tissues. Furthermore, their intense rate of activity makes them beguiling creatures to observe, as I've often discovered on warm winter days when I sit in the woods and watch the shrews popping in and out of the leaf litter in their frantic search for enough food to keep their extremely high metabolisms satisfied.

The nature center is open according to staff availability during the week most of the year, so it is best to call ahead 412-593-6105 for the current hours for the time of year you plan to visit. They also have free nature programs on the weekends, in season. Small groups also must arrange by calling ahead.

There is a picnic table at the nature center, but after a full morning watching the bird-banding, looking at the then inactive Sherman live-shrew traps, visiting the museum, and walking the nature trail, a better choice is to drive to nearby Linn Run State Park to use their picnic facilities and to hike the lovely one-mile circuit, Adam Falls Trail, that starts at the picnic area.

The large hemlock trees along Linn Run are lively with migrating warblers, including the northern parula, and the combination of the organized research-nature center and the little-developed state park provided a pleasing overview of the justly famous Laurel Highlands in southwestern Pennsylvania.

From Johnstown: Follow Pa. 271 southwest 20 miles to the intersection with Pa. 711. Turn left and follow 711 into Ligonier. Continue straight through the town to the intersection with U.S. 30. Turn left (east) on Route 30 and follow it 2 miles to the intersection with Pa. 381. Turn right (south) on 381. A sign for Linn Run State Park marks the intersection. Continue south on 381 for 6.3 miles from Route 30 to the nature center on the right.

To return to Linn Run State Park: Drive back (north) 2.3 miles from Route 30 and turn right on Linn Run Road, prominently marked by the state park sign. Drive 1.9 miles farther up the road, to the Adam Falls picnic area on the left.

49   QUEBEC RUN WILD AREA

If a wild area is defined as a place where you neither hear nor see any signs of civilization during an entire day's walk, then Quebec Run qualifies. Located in southern Forbes State Forest on the eastern slope of Chestnut Ridge, this 7,356-acre wild area in Fayette County has been purchased piecemeal by the Western Pennsylvania Conservancy and then turned over to the Pennsylvania Bureau of Forestry. The most recent acquisition—a 793-acre tract adjacent to the Quebec Run Wild Area to the west, and part of the Laurel Run watershed—contains one of only two known populations of white monkshood (*Aconitum reclinatum*) in the common-

Quebec Run. Quebec Run Wild Area.

wealth. A tall, slender herb with deeply divided leaves and an elongated cluster of helmet-shaped white flowers at the summit of the stem, white monkshood is not only state endangered but also a globally rare plant.

One of the best times to visit Quebec Run Wild Area is a sparkling day in mid-May, when you might be greeted by the song of a solitary vireo as you start to follow the blue-blazed Miller Trail to the east of the parking lot. At first the forest consists primarily of hardwoods, such as red oak, sugar maple, and black cherry, with an understory of mountain laurel and low-bush blueberry and wintergreen. But here and there a hemlock or rhododendron grows in solitary splendor. Then, as the ridge narrows and steepens after half a mile, the trail descends into a lowland forest of hemlock trees through a tunnel of large rhododendron shrubs.

Once you reach the flat floodplain of Mill Run, you will find yourself in a wildflower garden. There you can profitably spend an hour or more exploring the hemlock- and rhododendron-lined banks of pristine Mill Run, totting up the wildflower species, and trying to identify the bird calls you hear. Such birds as ovenbirds, scarlet tanagers, blue-gray gnatcatchers, and black-throated green warblers compete with the wind soughing in the trees, the chittering of chipmunks, and the crashing of deer in the underbrush.

The wildflowers include abundant skunk cabbage, along with the equally large leaves of false hellebore or Indian poke, growing beside Mill Run. Skunk cabbage blooms in March, and the large clusters of yellow-green, star-shaped false hellebore flowers open in June, but in May both plants provide a lush, leafy-green background for the smaller, May-blooming flowers—large-flowered trilliums, foamflowers, perfoliate bellworts, jack-in-the-pulpits, and halberd-leaved violets. Showiest of all are the blossoms of deep-pink, five-petaled smooth phlox. Another handsome flower is dwarf ginseng, with its rounded umbel of flowers overtopping a whorl of three stalked leaves, each with three leaflets.

Dwarf ginseng should not be confused with ginseng, its highly sought-after close relative. Although they share the same genus name, *Panax*, meaning "all remedy," which refers to the purported medicinal benefits of ginseng, their species' names—*trifolius* (three-leaved), for dwarf ginseng, and *quinquefolius* (five-leaved), for ginseng—provide an easy way to distinguish one plant from the other. Dwarf ginseng also has a round tuber, not a forking tuber as ginseng does. In addition, the flower of dwarf ginseng is white, and its fruit is a cluster of red berries, while ginseng has a pale yellow-green flower and a single yellow berry.

Finally, turn right onto Mill Run Trail, rock-hopping over a tiny tributary of Mill Run overhung with hemlock and rhododendron and buzzing with trunk-climbing black-and-white warblers. Along that trail, look for another showy wildflower—the vinelike swamp buttercup, which has shiny yellow petals and three segmented, toothy-edged leaves.

Shortly before reaching Rankin Trail, you pass an area of moss-covered downed trees, all of which have fallen naturally in the same direction, probably pushed over by a strong west wind. After turning right on the Rankin Trail, carefully cross Quebec Run over a pair of parallel, flat-sided logs. There is some evidence of beaver work in this area, as well as remnants of old dam works across the narrow, native trout-filled Quebec Run.

The blue-blazed Rankin Trail heads west more or less paralleling Quebec Run most of its length, and often you can look down at its rushing waters. Eventually you will cross Quebec Road. At this halfway point, you can turn right and take a shortcut back to your car, but a more scenic return is to continue on the trail after it crosses the road.

Then Rankin Trail makes a sharp jog to the right and follows the hillside. During this stretch, the stream is hidden from the trail above, so it is necessary to walk into the underbrush to your left and peer down through the rhododendron to see the rapids and miniature waterfalls of Quebec Run. To the right of the trail, look for massive sandstone boulders covered with liverworts and moss, which provide anchorage for sizable hemlocks and rhododendrons. On the day we visited, an added attraction was the mass migration of black-throated blue warblers throughout the rocky woods.

Finally you will reach the second sign for Hess Trail, which leads steeply uphill out of the Quebec Run stream valley and back into a mostly young hardwood forest, which the Western Pennsylvania Conservancy estimates was timbered about 1940. When the trail levels out, look for remnants of old timbered structures off the hill to your right—the remains of the only gold mine in Pennsylvania. In this forest, still leafless in mid-May, seeing migrating birds—solitary vireos, Blackburnian warblers, black-and-white warblers, and red-eyed vireos—is especially easy.

A final dip down to cross the headwaters of a Mill Run tributary over rocky terrain, and you finish back at the parking lot. Altogether you will have walked 4.5 miles and spent a day of solitude and beauty in this remote spot.

From Uniontown: Proceed east on U.S. 40 for 3.6 miles to the top of Chestnut Ridge. Turn right at the Mount Summit Inn onto Seaton Road, where the sign says "Laurel Caverns." Drive 6.4 miles until the main road takes a sharp right downhill—but do not take that road. Instead, proceed straight ahead on a rough, gravel road, Mud Pike Road. After 1.3 miles, turn right into the parking area for Quebec Run Wild Area.

SELECTED BIBLIOGRAPHY

Aron, Jean. *The Short Hiker: The Unicorn Hunter's Guide to Gentle Trails in Central Penn's Woods*. State College, Pa.: n.p., 1982 (revised 1987; revised second edition 1994).

Bonta, Marcia. *Outbound Journeys in Pennsylvania: A Guide to Natural Places for Individual and Group Outings*. University Park: The Pennsylvania State University Press, 1987 (revised 1990).

Brauning, Daniel W., ed. *Atlas of Breeding Birds in Pennsylvania*. Pittsburgh: University of Pittsburgh Press, 1992.

Cobb, Boughton. *A Field Guide to the Ferns*. Boston: Houghton Mifflin, 1956.

Dann, Kevin T. *Traces on the Appalachians: A Natural History of Serpentine in Eastern North America*. New Brunswick, N.J.: Rutgers University Press, 1988.

Durant, Mary. *Who Named the Daisy? Who Named the Rose? A Roving Dictionary of North American Wild Flowers*. New York: Dodd, Mead & Co., 1976.

Erdman, Dr. Kimball S., and Paul G. Weigman. *Preliminary List of Natural Areas in Pennsylvania*. Pittsburgh: Western Pennsylvania Conservancy, 1974.

Geyer, Alan R., and William H. Bolles. *Outstanding Scenic Geological Features of Pennsylvania*. Harrisburg, Pa.: Bureau of Topographic and Geologic Survey, 1979.

Grimm, William Carey. *The Shrubs of Pennsylvania*. Harrisburg, Pa.: Stackpole & Heck, 1952.

———. *The Trees of Pennsylvania*. Harrisburg, Pa.: Stackpole & Heck, 1950.

Harned, Joseph. *Wildflowers of the Alleghanies*. Oakland, Md.: n.p., 1936.

Harris, Larry D. *The Fragmented Forest: Island Biogeography and the Preservation of Biotic Diversity*. Chicago: University of Chicago Press, 1984.

Heintzelman, Donald S. *A Guide to Hawk Watching in North America*. University Park: The Pennsylvania State University Press, 1979.

Hoffmann, Carolyn. *Fifty Hikes in Eastern Pennsylvania: Day Hikes and Backpacks from the Susquehanna to the Poconos*. Second edition. Woodstock, Vt.: Backcountry Publications, 1989.

Johnson, Charles W. *Bogs of the Northeast*. Hanover, N.H.: University Press of New England, 1985.

Lawrence, Susannah, and Barbara Gross. *The Audubon Society Field Guide to the Natural Places of the Mid-Atlantic States: Inland*. New York: Pantheon Books, 1984.

Maser, Chris. *Forest Primeval: The Natural History of an Ancient Forest*. San Francisco: Sierra Club Books, 1989.

Merritt, Joseph F. *Guide to the Mammals of Pennsylvania*. Pittsburgh: University of Pittsburgh Press, 1987.

Mohlenbrock, Robert H. *Where Have All the Wildflowers Gone? A Region-by-Region*

Guide to Threatened or Endangered U.S. Wildflowers. New York: Macmillan, 1983.

Niering, William A. *The Life of the Marsh.* New York: McGraw-Hill, 1966.

Oplinger, Carl S., and Robert Halma. *The Poconos: An Illustrated Natural History Guide.* New Brunswick, N.J.: Rutgers University Press, 1988.

Palmer, Tim. *Rivers of Pennsylvania.* University Park: The Pennsylvania State University Press, 1980.

Peattie, Donald Culross. *A Natural History of Trees of Eastern and Central North America.* Second edition. New York: Bonanza Books, 1966.

Peterson, Roger Tory. *A Field Guide to the Birds.* Boston: Houghton Mifflin, 1980.

Peterson, Roger Tory, and Margaret McKenny. *A Field Guide to Wildflowers of Northeastern and Northcentral North America.* Boston: Houghton Mifflin, 1968.

Randour, Bill, and Alan Van Dine, eds. *Fifty Years of the Western Pennsylvania Conservancy.* Pittsburgh: Western Pennsylvania Conservancy, 1982.

Rhoads, Ann F., and William M. Klein Jr. *The Vascular Flora of Pennsylvania: Annotated Checklist and Atlas.* Philadelphia: American Philosophical Society, 1993.

Schafer, Jim, and Mike Sajna. *The Allegheny River: Watershed of the Nation.* University Park: The Pennsylvania State University Press, 1992.

Scott, Jane. *Botany in the Field: An Introduction to Plant Communities for the Amateur Naturalist.* Englewood Cliffs, N.J.: Prentice-Hall, 1984.

Shaffer, Larry L. *Pennsylvania Amphibians and Reptiles.* Harrisburg: Pennsylvania Fish Commission, 1991.

Thwaites, Tom. *Fifty Hikes in Central Pennsylvania: Day Hikes and Backpacking Trips in the Heart of the Keystone State.* Second edition. Woodstock, Vt.: Backcountry Publications, 1985.

————. *Fifty Hikes in Western Pennsylvania: Walks and Day Hikes from the Laurel Highlands to Lake Erie.* Second edition. Woodstock, Vt.: Backcountry Publications, 1990.

Van Diver, Bradford B. *Roadside Geology of Pennsylvania.* Missoula, Mont.: Mountain Press Publishing Company, 1990.